D1152748

Doing Your Dissertation *in* Business *and* Management

26 0147796 4

SAGE Study Skills

Doing Your Dissertation *in* Business *and* Management
The Reality of Researching and Writing

Reva Berman Brown

⑤SAGE Publications
London • Thousand Oaks • New Delhi

© Reva Berman Brown 2006

First published 2006

Apart from any fair dealing for the purposes of research or
private study, or criticism or review, as permitted under
the Copyright, Designs and Patents Act, 1988, this publication
may be reproduced, stored or transmitted in any form,
or by any means, only with the prior permission in writing
of the publishers, or in the case of reprographic reproduction,
in accordance with the terms of licences issued by the
Copyright Licensing Agency. Enquiries concerning
reproduction outside those terms should be sent to the
publishers.

 SAGE Publications Ltd
1 Oliver's Yard
55 City Road
London EC1Y 1SP

SAGE Publications Inc.
2455 Teller Road
Thousand Oaks, California 91320

SAGE Publications India Pvt Ltd
B-42, Panchsheel Enclave
Post Box 4109
New Delhi 110 017

British Library Cataloguing in Publication data

A catalogue record for this book is available
from the British Library

ISBN-10 1-4129-0350-5   ISBN-13 978-1-4129-0350-9
ISBN-10 1-4129-0351-3   ISBN-13 978-1-4129-0351-6 (pbk)

Library of Congress Control Number: 2005928564

Typeset by C&M Digitals (P) Ltd., Chennai, India
Printed and bound in Great Britain by TJ International Ltd, Padstow, Cornwall
Printed on paper from sustainable resources

Contents

1 What's in this for you?

Why the book was written

Why yet another book about researching and your Masters dissertation? Because this one will enable you to get much more out of all those other research methods books that you will encounter during your researching for your dissertation. It is intended to increase the satisfaction, pleasure and success that you gain from doing your dissertation.

It is an open secret that researching is not the logical, linear process that your research methods textbook suggests it is. It is also obvious that academic research is only different in degree and not in substance from what we do in our normal lives. Any decision you make, however trivial or important, requires you to research – why has the parcel not arrived? What is the best way to find out about scholarships? When will the results come out? Where did I put the car keys? Which new pair of trainers shall I get? Who can I ask to tell me about that? How can I avoid having to go there? In general, you clarify what it is you are intending to buy or do, find out what there is available, balance your options, evaluate your alternatives, and pick the one that suits you.

Sometimes you are more conscious of this process than on other occasions, but in the main, if asked afterwards, you can explain how you reached your choice – and it becomes apparent that, at whatever level of simplicity or complexity, you have researched it.

And if you think further, you realise that you didn't always do one thing after another – clarify, find out, balance, evaluate and choose. While you were thinking about those trainers or that job, you were simultaneously evaluating the information you already had, as well as searching out more. You may well have already chosen, and then used the various decision processes to explain or justify your choice to yourself.

Academic research is a specialised part of ordinary life, not something totally removed from it. Research methods books are written in the way that they are because you need the information they contain, and you need to know one thing after another so that you can use that knowledge to do a lot of things at the same time.

This book points out which of those things need to be done at the same time, so that you can bring your ordinary-life skills of simultaneous action to research and produce your dissertation.

The number of Masters level degrees in business and management (MA, MSc, and MBA) is increasing. Each of these degrees requires a dissertation or project resulting from research undertaken by the student. One could number the books which supply research methods for this component of Masters programmes in double, if not treble figures.

All of these books provide advice on how to do a dissertation, listing the research issues – the different research approaches available, specific methods for data collection and analysis, the writing-up stage. Although many research methods books acknowledge that research tasks are carried out simultaneously, for the sake of clarity, the books tend to present the tasks in a sequential manner, as though the researcher begins at the obvious beginning with a research problem and proceeds through the steps suggested to produce the finished document.

It is well-known by all researchers (novice or experienced) that research is not undertaken in that way – that different activities are often performed in parallel and not sequentially, and that the writing-up is not conducted in the order in which the dissertation or thesis is finally presented.

This book is not intended to replace the research methods textbooks that your supervisor has recommended. It supplements these, and fills out the information they supply by explaining how a dissertation is really researched and written, in all its chaos and uncertainty.

The book is written in 'easy English' rather than 'academic-speak' and deals in a straightforward manner with all the phases of undertaking a Masters dissertation, covering how to lay a foundation for the project, find a research problem, develop a proposal, and how to organise and write each chapter.

Its distinctive feature is that it does not treat the research process as a linear progression from a clear beginning to the end, but deals with the topics in the simultaneous order in which they are undertaken, rather than the order which is implied in current research methods books.

It starts before the beginning, assisting you to clarify your thoughts about yourself as a researcher and then about the project ahead of you. It therefore:

- **deals in more detail with the issues of finding the topic than is often provided in research methods books**

- **explains what is behind the requirements involved in creating the research proposal**

- **gives advice on the actual process of writing**

- **is a practical, down-to-earth user's manual intended to tell it how it is, not how it should be.**

What the book will achieve for your supervisors

The book will:

- save them hours of repeating themselves in giving advice and encouragement when students come individually with the same problems and difficulties

- help them to be better supervisors – in writing the book, I have made explicit a number of items which supervisors sometimes take for granted because 'surely everybody knows that?', when everybody doesn't necessarily know it

- provide them with the satisfaction that comes from knowing that they have been able to provide advice and assistance to more students than those they currently teach.

What the book will achieve for you

The book will:

- help you to find the topic that you intend to research

- explain why you need to create the research proposal, so you understand why you are often made to do one

- support you through the confusion and anxiety that is a normal companion to undertaking research

- explain why you need to write your dissertation in a style that is often difficult to use

- advise you on the actual process of writing

- tell you how research for your dissertation is actually done, not how it should be done

- enable you to become a member of the community of researchers into management and organisations by introducing you to the real, as opposed to the ideal, world of research.

What the book does not do

It does not:

- present research as a linear, systematic, totally rational process that, once planned, can be conducted in a smooth, coherent flow, with no hitches, accidents or obstacles

- use 'academic-speak'

- repeat what is well-covered in current research methods textbooks such as detailed explanations of methods of data collection or data analysis

- explain the conventions or technicalities of referencing

- suggest learning outcomes

- solve all your researching problems

- replace the need to use your research methods textbook

- give lists of all the other books, papers and articles you should refer to as well as reading this one.

It is thus not a stand-alone research methods book, but is intended to supplement these types of books with the actual process that is undertaken by all researchers – doing things in parallel, jumping backwards and forwards in both process and substance, creating order out of the chaos and uncertainty of researching.

How to use the book

I suggest that you read the book from start to finish. It won't take you long, and the time you spend reading it may well save you far more time when you come to do your research. Then, when your dissertation reaches the point where one of the chapters would be helpful, have another read to remind yourself of the information and tips that I've provided to guide and help you on your way to your research destination.

Something to bear in mind

When you start out on the research adventure, it might be helpful to bear in mind that despite all the emphasis on the systematic, scientific and the rigorous, research is essentially a human activity, affected by passions, hopes, imagination, cultural biases and personal prejudices.

The payoff

Research may be a serious endeavour, but it is also exciting and fun and very worthwhile. If you follow the advice in this book, what's in it for you is a better dissertation than you would have researched and written if you hadn't given any of this a moment's thought.

2 Before you begin to begin

Where do you stand?

Before you can begin to research, you need to know certain things, the first of which is the kind of researcher you are. This will affect everything from recognising the research problem to the way you undertake the research to the way that you write it up.

If you have been provided with a research methods course during your Masters programme, you will have been introduced to an alien vocabulary – ontology, epistemology, axiology, paradigm, positivist, phenomenological – describing concepts that in themselves are complex but not complicated, and about which you may already have thought, but not in those words.

But for those specialised words to make sense to you, you need to recognise their relevance to you as a researcher.

When you have given some thought to the information provided in this chapter, you will be in a better position to assess what kind of dissertation will work for you. I talk you through the various kinds, leading to a description of what to expect of a research proposal and the other things you need to think about at the outset. Remember that you are aiming for a well-written dissertation, and writing well emerges from clear thinking – and that, in turn, depends on clear understanding of what you are doing, and why you are doing it.

What kind of a researcher are you?

In the main, there are five broad types of researcher, which I call the detective, the doctor, the explorer, the insider and the outsider. These are what the textbooks call 'ideal types' – the perfect example that doesn't actually exist in our imperfect world.

The researcher as detective

 A detective is a person who solves crimes from the uncovering of clues. The researcher as detective solves problems from the discovery of indicators relevant to the problem. The researcher detective knows what the research problem is – why is absenteeism so high in firm X?, what happened to make that change programme go so horribly wrong?, when did firm Y begin to show signs of being in trouble?, where can firm Z find more suppliers of raw materials?, which is the best computer system to buy?, who was responsible for that decision?, how do effective teams produce their output? – and needs to uncover and discover the clues that will solve the problem. (Chapter 4 deals in more detail with the issue of the research problem.) The clues then need to be put together in the form of evidence, so that others are convinced that the correct solution to the research puzzle has been found.

The researcher as doctor

 The doctor is presented with a variety of symptoms, and has to diagnose the disease before the appropriate medication can be prescribed. The researcher as doctor is aware of symptoms – the high absenteeism in a firm, the resistance to a change process, the atmosphere of stress and tension in a department – and needs to diagnose what is ailing the firm, so as to prescribe appropriate medicine that will work and cure the problem. The researcher doctor is concerned to find the reasons behind the research question.

The researcher as explorer

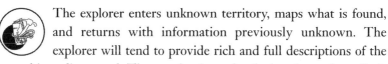 The explorer enters unknown territory, maps what is found, and returns with information previously unknown. The explorer will tend to provide rich and full descriptions of the new things discovered. The use that is made of what the explorer finds is generally not the explorer's concern, which is about novelty, and first-time knowledge. Often, it is the journey itself, into and through the unknown, that is of higher value than any of the discoveries made while exploring. The story of the exploration is what holds the reader's interest, with the description of the discoveries taking a less significant place in the narrative – whoever the readers might be – your supervisor(s), your examiner(s), or other Masters students.

The hybrid researcher

Whichever ideal type you are closest to, it is more likely that you will approach research with aspects of all of them. It may be that your research problem requires 'detective' skills at the beginning, but then moves on to need 'doctor' skills in order to provide as complete a solution as possible.

But it is nevertheless helpful to bring to the front of your mind the researcher type which is your dominant approach. It will make it easier to choose your topic and to conduct your research if you know about your own researcher inclinations.

The researcher as insider

Separate from the ideal types, though it can be combined with them, is the issue of where you place yourself in the insider/outsider split. If you are involved in researching your own area of work in your place of employment, you are doing one of the two types of insider research. You are the truest insider in that you are examining yourself, your motives, your methods, your inputs and outputs, and the consequences (intended or not) of what you do. Not much research is undertaken in this mode in management and business as there are problems of lack of objectivity and bias that need more skill to resolve than a novice researcher like you can comfortably cope with.

The other type of insider research has you as the researcher trying to find out what is 'inside' the people you are researching. You are attempting to understand the thinking or behavioural patterns of people in organisations, in order to consider what they really mean when they say or do something. When undertaking this kind of research you might either be watching others, or be working beside them and watching them at the same time. You then have the ethical problem of whether or not to tell the people you are working alongside that you are watching what they do and say, with an ulterior motive of researching in mind.

Most insider research tends to be reported in narrative form. There are likely to be 'numbers' – percentages or ranges of counts – but these are minor aspects, supporting the narrative account.

The researcher as outsider

As an acknowledged outsider, someone who has come in from elsewhere to undertake research, you have freedoms and constraints that the insider does not share. You can also be an outsider even if you are involved in researching your own place of work, because, although you are inside the firm, you may be researching a part of the firm in which you do not work.

The outsider's viewpoint makes it easier to establish facts, rather than meanings, and to analyse them quantitatively, rather than explain them in a narrative format.

Research itself as inside or outside

The type of research that you do can also be inside (emic) or outside (etic). This distinction is one of the important issues in cross-cultural research. 'Inside' research approaches are concerned with how the 'inhabitants' conceptualise the world. The researcher studies behaviour from within the system, examines only one culture or system or procedure, using internal criteria to discover the structures being researched. 'Outside' (etic) research is more concerned with universals, so the behaviour is studied from a position outside the system, many cultures, systems or procedures are compared, and the criteria used to create the structures are considered to be absolute and universal.

What is your overall approach to research?

Which kind of researcher are you most comfortable being? You really need to know. While a great deal of research is conducted in a state of anxiety, if you aren't aware of yourself as a researcher, you may find yourself feeling even more on edge all the time you are planning and doing the research, because it doesn't fit properly with your natural way of investigating things.

You probably aren't the 'ideal type', but will like searching for clues, while also having an interest in travelling around unknown territory and, at the same time, watching out for the way the inhabitants of that region behave. But logic has it that you will have a preference, and you owe it to yourself to clarify what that preference for researching is before you begin to plan it.

Researcher type and dissertation type

While there is a common sense connection between the type of researcher you are and the type of dissertation you will be inclined to produce, this link can sometimes be somewhat unclear. For instance, the implication is that the Detective and the Doctor already know what the research problem is, while the Explorer may or may not know. These descriptions are therefore only aids to suggest routes to researcher self-definition.

Research strategy/methodology

If the author of your research methods textbook has been careful, he/she will have called the overall perspective or philosophy of researching by its proper name of 'methodology'. Confusion arises when either the textbook's author or your supervisor incorrectly calls the techniques of researching – your research methods – by the term 'methodology'. This can result in misunderstanding and confusion on both your parts.

Methodology is the philosophical framework within which the research is conducted, or the foundation upon which the research is based. You might also hear the phrase 'research strategy' used in place of 'methodology' and it means the same thing – the basic philosophical orientation of the research. Put another way, methodology is the rationale for the particular methods you use in your researching, and in that type of research in general. If your dissertation regulations require you to provide a section called methodology, then check whether you are being asked to explain the general approach you have adopted for defining your research problem, and for collecting your information and analysing or interpreting it, or whether you are expected to outline and justify the techniques you have used to collect your data.

You may be instructed to detail your methodology in your research proposal, and you will then correctly provide information about your views of reality, knowledge and values. But you may get the proposal flung back at you because 'you haven't mentioned your methodology', when it hasn't been made clear to you that this particular supervisor's interpretation of the word 'methodology' is inaccurate and you were supposed to list the specific techniques (like interviews) you will be using to collect your information, or the techniques (like tables of frequencies) you will be using to analyse the information once you have collected it.

Therefore, a word of warning here. Make sure that you and your supervisor are using the term 'methodology' in the same way – it will save endless hassle and wasted time and effort.

As I have suggested, your methodology is made up of three strands – considerations about what is real, what is knowledge or knowable, and what values underpin research. Because views about these three strands are not universally held, you need to know what your own views are so that you can explain where you are coming from, and, therefore, why your research has the 'shape' that it has.

Academics are accustomed to using the technical terms for their perspectives on reality (ontology), knowledge (epistemology) and values (axiology) and so you will be expected to use these terms instead of the more everyday words that are their equivalent.

Your methodology will tend to be either concerned with abstractions and concepts (theoretical) or concerned with facts and techniques (empirical). The two major divisions of empirical methodology are positivism and interpretivism. Your textbook should discuss these both as methodologies and also as research techniques. Positivism tends to lend itself towards undertaking research using quantitative techniques and interpretivism towards qualitative techniques. However, you will find that you will probably need both quantitative and qualitative techniques in order to progress your research.

Reality/Ontology

While we might have some difficulty in defining what we mean by 'real', we all know what is real when we come across it. But because your definition of reality may differ from other people you know, before you begin to research, you need to have the issue of 'the real' clear in your own mind. You are going to need to explain to your readers, either explicitly in so many words or implicitly in your dissertation's tone and perspective, where you are coming from. If you don't do so, readers of your dissertation may legitimately assume that their (possibly very different) view of reality is also yours. This misunderstanding can permeate the reading of your entire dissertation and result in an undervaluing of your research, and a subsequent lower evaluation of your contribution.

Put simply, reality is either 'out there' (objectively external to you), or 'in here' (subjectively within yourself), or it is 'in here' because it has been brought in from 'out there'. And it can get tricky because, while it is possible to justify a position about the material world and where it 'really' exists, it is more difficult to justify the reality of abstractions such as dreams or justice. It is clear that the view you take about what you consider to be real affects everything you do, including your research.

Knowledge/Epistemology

Assumptions about the nature of knowledge underpin any approach to research. If you don't consider something to be knowledge or to be worth knowing, it is logically then not worth researching. It is only common sense to say that research is about knowledge – research is about what you know, what you recognise as worth knowing, and what you do about the knowledge you have recognised as worth knowing.

While there are elements of the absurd or the ridiculous in the epistemology battles fought out between researchers and academics of different schools of thought, the matter is a serious one. The study of the grounds upon which knowledge is based influences recognition of its limits and validity.

A simple example: if you consider that reality is 'out there' and can be observed and counted, then knowledge is that which has been observed and counted, and anything else that cannot be observed or counted is logically not knowledge, or may even be impossible to know.

Values/Axiology

There was a time when social science research (of which business and management research is a part) was considered to be objective and value-free, that is, the personal values of the researcher aren't biased or prejudiced, and he or she doesn't undertake research with preconceived notions or foregone conclusions. The classic style of scientific research is that it is objective research, based on clear-cut academic disciplines. It is accepted that consultancy (sometimes called applied research), which researchers tend to be paid to undertake, has values and knowledge systems concerned with practical relevance. This is because, unlike classical scientific research, applied research is rooted in political and social contexts, and in the needs of practitioners.

What you will be doing, albeit unpaid, is applied research, and it is a value-laden, sometimes very political process. Some of those values will be your own, and some will be those of your organisation or supervisor which you might find expedient to adopt for the time being.

In your dissertation, while you don't need to be explicit about your values, you do need to be clear for yourself, what these values are. You may come across dubious practices in your research, for example, and you need to have an idea of what you intend to do about it.

For instance, one of my students discovered that his firm kept two sets of accounts, one for the Internal Revenue and tax-paying, and one for the owner of the firm and non-tax-paying. His response was to ignore this fact while doing his Masters (his boss was paying his fees and allowing him time to do his degree), and after he received his qualification, he left the firm. I don't know whether or not he reported the firm for its false accounting.

If you are asked to provide a paragraph about values, it is likely to be a statement that you are aware that you can't be entirely objective and impartial in your judgements, but that you are doing all you can to be as unbiased as you possibly can.

Ethics

Values naturally lead on to ethics. While you don't need to go overboard on the ethics issue – you are not going to be experimenting on someone who is sick or too young to understand what you are doing – you do need to think about the assorted ethical issues that your research will create. Approaching this from a negative point of view, the last thing you want is to be sued for alleged misconduct should the people who participate in your research feel that their rights and dignity have been infringed.

In a sense, ethical behaviour in research isn't complicated. You should avoid actions or questions that can be viewed as threats to your partici-pants' health, values or dignity. One of the ways to achieve this is to get the informed consent of your participants. Explain who you are –

a student undertaking research for a dissertation – what it is you are researching, and why you wish them to provide their views or opinions. They also need to know what you intend to do with the information that they provide, so that they can consent to that. Never deliberately mislead participants about the purpose or nature of the research. And your participants should be informed at the outset that they can withdraw from participating at any moment if they wish to do so. Indeed, they have the right to withdraw their consent retrospectively and to require you to destroy the data that you have collected with their participation. Let them know how to contact you, should they wish to do so after their participation.

Offer confidentiality and anonymity, and mean it. Do not disclose who your participants are without their specific permission to do so. If they have provided you with information that is personal and/or private, they must be given the genuine assurance that the information will be protected and they will not be identified as the provider of that information.

Your business school may have a formal requirement that you fill in a form about your ethical approach to your research which will be sent to a Research Officer or Research Committee to be approved before you can begin your data collection. You may need to build the time that this will take into your preparations.

Have a look at Appendix 2 which says a little more about the ethics issue.

Research

Before you begin to begin, you have two more chores to undertake. The first is to find out what your business school considers 'research' to be, and the second – dealt with in the next section – is to be sure what the business school means by 'dissertation'.

'Research' is simply another word for 'enquiry', though admittedly, it is a special kind of enquiry. Research is the process of systematically gathering and analysing or interpreting information in order to gain knowledge and understanding. Researching involves two skills which are based on normal, everyday human activities – talking to people or watching them – and you have already had a lifetime's experience of doing this.

Research into business and management frequently (though not always) focuses on people and their behaviour or attitudes. It tends to involve a specific question, decision or problem facing a specific organisation, and obtains information about these. It sometimes tests ideas about the causes of a problem and is a systematic way of achieving the understanding and information necessary for some decision or action that will result from what is discovered during the research process.

Student research

You are no doubt well aware that you are not an academic and that, while research is generally the same thing whether undertaken by a student or an experienced academic, there are constraints on you-as-student imposed by the particular environment in which you are working.

You are well aware that:

- **while you are ostensibly free to choose any topic that interests you, you may have a topic imposed on you because of the availability of supervisors and their interests and workloads**

- **your research has to be completed within strict deadlines, and extensions may be difficult to get**

- **within the time allotted for the research, you have to learn how to do it while actually doing it**

- for whatever reason, you don't get on with your supervisor, and you have to cope with the problems that brings

- you are not only expected to add to knowledge but also to demonstrate that you have acquired competence in undertaking research

- the degree of originality required of you is never really made clear.

The only comfort that I can give you is that these constraints are not only experienced by all Masters students, but they are also overcome, admittedly sometimes with great effort, but overcome and triumphed over, nevertheless.

3 On the edge of beginning

Defining the dissertation

There are a number of different types of dissertation that your business school might be willing to accept as appropriate for your course. They will tend to define these in academic-speak, for example:

1. The traditional dissertation

An empirical investigation, based on primary and/or secondary data, of a management or organisational practice, justified and supported by detailed reference to relevant theories and concepts from the literature.

What they are talking about is the 'traditional' dissertation. To simplify, it is research resulting from looking at a problem or practice in a place of work – absenteeism, supply chain difficulties, recruitment, motivation, flexible working practices – and 'explaining' it in terms of the theories that you have been taught. This type of dissertation is likely to require you to provide recommendations for the solution of the problem or improvement of the practice investigated.

Part-time students who are being sponsored by their employers often find that the subject of their dissertation is handed to them by their line manager, because the solution to the problem or removal of the difficulty would benefit the organisation. If this is the case, then this is the type of dissertation that will satisfy both the business school that is giving you your qualification and your employer, who is either paying your fees or giving you time off to attend the course, or both.

Another reason why this is the most common type of dissertation is that having your organisation's support to undertake it will eliminate any problems of access to the information you need. And you don't need to be a genius to work out that no data means no dissertation, and thus no Masters.

Another type of dissertation is similar to the one described above. Again, in academic-speak:

2. The test-a-model dissertation

The empirical testing and development of an existing management model or the development of a new model, with data contributing to the conceptual aspects of this model, justified and supported by detailed reference to relevant theories and concepts from the literature.

Here, you take something from the literature – for example, a model of strategic planning or of customer retention – and, drawing on relevant theory, you test the model in your place of work/an organisation. The result will be not so much recommendations for improvement of organisational practices as confirmation or disconfirmation of the effectiveness or reliability of the model to explain the theoretical concept on which it is based.

A third type of dissertation approaches the same area as the second one, but from a different angle.

3. The applying-the-theory dissertation

The application of relevant theories and concepts to the solving of a managerial or organisational problem, where practical recommendations arise from the interactions between theories and concepts from the literature and the data collected.

In this type of dissertation, you take a theory – for example, the expectancy theory of motivation or the theory of cultural diffusion – and apply the theory to a problem in the workplace in order to explain what is going on there. So, for instance, you will give an explanation of an apparent lack of motivation in the despatch department of an organisation in terms of expectancy theory, and you will then go on to recommend improvements, using the theory and what you have read in the literature.

The second and third types of dissertation are two sides of the same coin. In one, you take a problem and explain it in terms of existing theory (or the new theory that you have developed during your research) and in the other, you take the theory and justify it in terms of the interaction between data you have collected and the literature existing on the topic.

The fourth type of dissertation initially sounds easy to do, but actually requires a great deal of intellectual effort.

4. The literature review dissertation

A thorough analytical review of the literature of a given field, indicating that the student has complete, up-to-date knowledge of the field and has been able to comment on, discuss, compare, contrast and criticise what has been published in the area over a defined number of years.

The problem when undertaking this type of dissertation is that just describing in a one-thing-after-another fashion won't result in an acceptable dissertation. There is nothing gained by saying that this author wrote the first paper about the issue in 1962, which said A, B and C, and then that author wrote the next important paper in 1968, which said A, B, C,

D and E, and so on into the present. What you are after is to say that this author wrote the first paper about the issue in 1962, which said A, B and C. These ideas were found interesting and were subsequently researched by others. And then, the author of the next important paper in 1968, confirmed that A, B, C are valid explanations of the issue, and then added D and E as developments/improvements of the original arguments.

It isn't all that easy to comment on, discuss, compare, contrast and criticise what has been published in the area over a defined number of years. For this literature review type of dissertation, you are required to show that you are thoroughly conversant with what has been written on the topic and that you are able to discuss the issues in an analytical and critical manner, using informed judgement to justify your expressed opinions.

For those of you who would really rather not undertake research using 'real people', and having to approach them directly in interviews or indirectly via questionnaires, this kind of dissertation is a life-saver. You can sit quietly and read without having problems of access and the political issues that are sometimes involved in empirical research.

The fifth type of dissertation is different from the others in that it does not collect data from living people, and it is concerned with a more distant past than the very recent past or the present with which the other types of dissertation are involved.

5. The historical investigation dissertation

An historical investigation of a managerial/organisational theory, concept or practice showing its development and changes over a specified period with detailed reference to relevant literature.

There is a view that theory is ahistorical. The word means that it is outside time, existing unchanging in some abstract place available for tapping into whenever wanted. Logic will tell you that this isn't the case, and that theory is a result of the time and circumstances in which it is proposed. This is because research itself is based in circumstances occurring at the time of the research. For example, if the economy is booming, it is unlikely that people will undertake research into the causes or possible outcomes of the non-existent recession. If an area is seen as no longer interesting, little research is undertaken in it – if only because such research won't contribute to furthering an academic's career.

So, investigating how and why a particular theory, concept or practice came to start, and then developed in importance – and then possibly died a death and was abandoned – is both interesting and a fruitful contribution to knowledge. For instance, at one point Management by Objectives was the 'in' thing and was recommended by researchers and consultants as an effective way to manage. Now it is sometimes taught in business schools, but is mostly ignored. Or, in the 1980s, organisational climate was an exciting area to research. Then organisational culture took over, and the majority of climate researchers became culture researchers, and climate was left to a minority of those still interested enough in it to continue to research it.

In general, there are two main perspectives to researching and each affects what you do and how you do it.

1. Historical perspective

Research undertaken with a historical perspective is concerned with identifying how something has changed over time – or how (and why) it has stayed the same despite the passing of time. And, of course, 'time' means whatever you wish or need it to mean – years, decades, centuries or days, weeks and months. The historical perspective involves the kinds of events that the research focuses on, the time period covered, and the type of contribution the research intends to make.

This kind of research will often contain its limits within the title:

- **The development of supply change management 1970–1980**

- **The rise and fall of British manufacturing in the 20th century**

- **Transitions in the definition of the entrepreneur from 1985 to 2005**

- **Succession planning in family firms – the past 100 years.**

If you do this kind of research, bear in mind that just simply telling the story is not enough. You are going to need to explain, analyse, criticise, comment on, and evaluate the topic.

2. Present-focused perspective

Research with a present-focused perspective is interested in the present condition of whatever is being investigated. In the main, this kind of research is concerned with patterns of characteristics, attitudes or events. Data collection can be by means of interviews so that verbal portrayals or expositions are collected, or by means of questionnaires so as to collect information in terms of amounts and frequencies.

Reporting present-focused research is often done in the form of case studies, for example:

- **Celebrating retirement in Azimov Bakeries**

- **The daily lives of receptionists in a medical practice**

- **Selling the product – the case of Bix Enterprises.**

If you have participated in the activities of the people, organisation or event that you investigated, then you have undertaken a type of study called an ethnography. Its main use is to provide understanding of the structure and inner workings of a group. The contrast between a case study and an ethnography is that the case study tends to reveal the individualistic attributes of a particular person, organisation or event, and ethnographies identify beliefs and customs shared by a social system of some kind, which can range from a work team to an entire organisation. Put simplistically, case studies emphasise the things that make one person or organisation different from others, and ethnographies emphasise the commonalities that unify members of a group. Examples of ethnographic studies are:

- **shadowing solicitors in a legal firm**

- **going out with an ambulance crew**

- **working on an assembly line.**

Present-status research undertaken quantitatively generally uses surveys, and experiments to collect data, and various statistical procedures to analyse them. These can range from simple counting of amounts, frequencies and correlations (what happens to Something A when Something B changes?) to sophisticated techniques such as discriminant analysis and multiple regression.

Experiments can be carried out in management and business research, though this is a research method rarely used. Experiments entail treating objects in a strictly defined way and then evaluating the outcome to decide how the treatment influenced the objects, and why the treatment had that effect. You could conduct an experiment, for instance, to find out how a series of training videos about business ethics influence employees' views about their own ethical business behaviour. This kind of thing needs skill to plan, undertake, analyse and evaluate, and the time constraints of the average Masters dissertation make experiments one of the more difficult types of research to do.

Double-checking on the requirements

So here is the most important thing that you need to clarify before you begin to begin. Make absolutely sure what your business school means when it says you are required to undertake a dissertation. And then, once it is clear to you, you can put this information together with your understanding of the kind of researcher you are, and your views about reality, knowledge, values, human nature, and ethics. And you have all you need to know in order to begin the process that will result in your dissertation.

Skills you will need

How you undertake and write up both your research proposal and your dissertation depends on the type of dissertation you choose to do. Whether you are doing the 'traditional dissertation' or one of the other, less common types, you will need to sharpen the skills required to carry out the research posed by your problem.

For writing your proposal, you will need to be able to clarify your thinking and to crystallise in writing the significant aspects of tasks that will seem to you, as yet, very indistinct and poorly formed. Nevertheless, hard thinking now will save you much time later.

The one thing they will all have in common is that the proposal is written in the future tense. You are, after all, explaining what you propose to do when you begin your research. In the main, if the proposal is sufficiently detailed and thought out, you will be able to use it as your Research Design section, only this time, you put it in the past tense, because you are explaining how you did the research.

1. Designing research

There are literally hundreds of books on the market that will instruct you on how to design your research. Another source of help is your tutors and supervisor. The practical skills are easy to learn. It is the more intangible skills that are difficult to teach. You will need somehow to absorb these more intellectual research skills by discussion, thinking, reflection or even the use of your imagination. What you are after can best be defined as a 'feel' for the best or most appropriate way to design the research process. All I can say is 'Trust your intuition'. If it feels right, it more than likely is the right way to go.

2. Developing research instruments

The tools – questionnaires or interview schedules – you will use to gather the information that you need are called research instruments in academic-speak. Creating either of them is a specialised skill, and you have a choice of two alternatives. Either you need to put in time learning how to create a questionnaire or an interview schedule so that it asks exactly what you need to know without wasting your respondent's or interviewee's time when answering, or you could take care to formulate a research problem that can be solved by using standardised or previously developed instruments. There are a number of books that include already developed and tested questionnaires and you could either use these as-is, or you could adapt them for your own research needs. Of course, you will have to acknowledge that you have done so, citing name(s) of whoever it was who first devised and tested the questionnaire, otherwise you will be plagiarising.

3. Collecting data

These skills are relatively easily acquired and my advice is that you prac-tise on others, family members or fellow students, before launching yourself into the real world. You only have one chance to collect your data, and if you mess up an interview, or can't persuade the people-who-have-the-answers to respond to your questionnaire, rescuing your pro-ject from disaster is not guaranteed. And, of course, before collecting your data, it will benefit you to have given some serious thought to the amount of data that you require. This is a difficult one – how many questionnaires or interviews are 'enough'? Your supervisor should be able to advise you on what, for your purposes, is an adequate number of questionnaires to send out or interviews to undertake.

Developing a questionnaire or interview schedule requires two kinds of skill. The first concerns what you decide to ask and how you decide you will ask it, but you need a further skill – the ability to think about how you intend to analyse the information that the questionnaire or interview schedule will produce at the same time as you are developing them. It isn't enough to have the skill to create an appropriate question. You need the skill of knowing how you intend to deal with the answer.

4. Analysing data

This is the most difficult bit for the inexperienced researcher as analysis skills are specialised. As a result, you need to consult your supervisor on the implication for data analysis of your research problem. Now that there are computer programs that will do the calculations for you, statistical tests aren't difficult to run. The difficulty lies in interpreting what the 'numbers' tell you. Again, there are a great number of books on using statistics to analyse research, and your supervisor will be able to guide you in choosing the appropriate ones.

To simplify and generalise, what the computer programs will be able to test for – and this is both for quantitative and qualitative research – are relationships between whatever it is you are looking at or looking for, or differences between them.

5. Writing research

Skills in research writing are essential. It would be a tragedy to spoil all your effort and hard work by presenting a dissertation that is badly or inappropriately or confusingly written.

The last chapter goes into more detail about academic writing and how to develop enough skill to enable you to use this specialised 'language'. Suffice it to say here, that this particular skill is indispensable. Truth be told, academic life being what it is, and academics being what they are, you are more likely to succeed with a relatively shallow piece of work written with flair and panache, than a solid piece of work that is stodgy and boring to read.

Research proposal – why is it needed?

If you have undertaken the typical Masters degree, you will have spent over half of the academic year taking courses that are examined. The one that is different is the Research Methods course which is intended to introduce you to the world of researching. If it is assessed, then the thing to be assessed is going to be the Research Proposal. The assessment serves a number of purposes – it checks that you have grasped the rudiments of research, and it requires you to formalise your research intentions and to write these down. The knowledge that you will have to produce a research proposal may lead you to think about what the subject of your dissertation is likely to be some months before your study course requires you to do so.

It often happens that in the course of learning about some field about which, initially, you knew very little – say marketing, when before undertaking the Masters, your work was in human resource management or strategy – you come across something that sparks off an interest, and you decide that this area is the one you will research for your dissertation.

If you have indeed been sporadically thinking about the area or the topic that interests you in the months prior to the point where you have to put your research proposal together, you will have far less hassle to contend with than if you leave the decision about what to research until the very last moment.

What is sometimes ignored in the process of creating the research proposal is that one of its functions is to form a kind of provisional agreement between you and your supervisor – and the business school – concerning your aims and your supervisor's commitment to helping you achieve these. Of course, a research proposal does not form a binding contract, and you can change its contents after it has been approved, but at least it has provided a specific map of the route you intend to follow to get you from the beginning of the research journey to the successful end.

If, after taking or enduring your research methods course, you are still undecided about your topic or unsure about the proposal, there are a number of Websites that will provide even more hints and tips. Instead of spoon-feeding you and giving you a long list of these Websites, I have mentioned their existence, and will leave you to test out your own researching skill in searching the Web for them.

Research proposal – what are its elements?

Now that you know what kind of dissertation your business school expects from you, you need to find out what type of research proposal is expected.

Academic research proposals are usually composed of specific elements, presented in a specific order:

- the title of the research to be undertaken

- the aims of the research

- the background of the research problem

- the research problem

- **the research design – overall approach to research and methods for data collection and analysis**

- **references**

- **timeline.**

Once you know what kind of dissertation your business school expects of you, and you have some understanding of why you need to prepare a proposal, you need to be clear on the expected format of your proposal – the sequence of elements – that are expected.

Title

The title will contain, in a few words, the essence of your research. It should accurately reflect your intentions at this preliminary stage. Another purpose of the title is that it is likely to contain the keywords that someone might use in an attempt to locate the kind of study you are proposing to do. A good title often has a structure that will progress from the general to the specific, for example 'The effectiveness of shopmobility schemes in six county towns in south-east England'.

The aims of the research

These are the heart of your project. If you can't state the aims of your research in two or three sentences or bullet points, then you probably haven't given sufficient thought to what you intend to do.

The background

You need to explain the context from which your research problem has emerged to the person who is going to read and evaluate your proposal.

Some of the factors which make up the context might be a building (for example, a prison or school), material goods (household products), a situation (interactions in an R&D department), or an organisation (your place of employment or a social club). Other contextual factors could well be more conceptual, and concern the local economy, educational policy, or legislation. Or the context could concern even more abstract issues and involve power, or control, or change.

This is one of the difficult bits of your proposal because you need to reference your argument with the work of previous researchers, and you probably won't have done much more than found out who the important authors and experts are, and what they have written. Nevertheless, you will need to place your proposed research into its context, and it will be accepted by the person who evaluates your proposal that you have only provided initial information about the relevant literature, and indeed, the nature of your research problem.

The research problem

This is the focus of your proposal, and it must be very clear what the nature of the problem is, and why it is significant enough to be researched. While you could express your problem in abstract terms, it is not acceptable to express it in general terms. It must be precisely defined so that it is obvious that you have limited the scope of your research to what is feasible and practical.

The research design

You need to explain what you are going to do in order to carry out your research, and why you are going to do whatever it is you have chosen to do. Your supervisor can advise you on the amount of detail wanted. Obviously, the methods you choose are going to be those which will allow you to collect and analyse your data effectively. You must mention issues of access to certain people or certain types of information.

References

You may be lucky to have a supervisor who is a dragon about referencing. Accurate referencing (and its sibling, citing) will provide your dissertation with more merit and approval than you might otherwise expect. It isn't all that difficult to learn how your business school prefers referencing to be laid out. There are a great many ways to set out references and because all of them are a matter of tradition or custom, all of them are right. You just need to find out which of all the variety of correct ways to reference your supervisor or business school considers to be the most right or the greatly preferred.

Another reason why you are a lucky student if your supervisor takes your referencing seriously is that by presenting accurate referencing you won't put your examiner into that hostile frame of mind where sloppy referencing is seen as slapdash thinking, which leads to careless researching, ending in untrustworthy results and a shoddy dissertation. None of which is going to benefit you in any way.

Bite the bullet, and even if you secretly think it is all smoke and mirrors, get your referencing as near to perfect as you possibly can – and then sit back and reap the benefits.

Timeline

This is necessary, and is also always going to be inaccurate, not only because you are going to misjudge the time it will take you to do things but also because, while your timeline is linear, your research process isn't (see Chapter 5).

But even assuming that you will undertake your research in a linear fashion, as a novice researcher you are unlikely to be accurate in your estimate of how long things will take. What your supervisor wants is an indication that you know what you need to do in order to accomplish your research and that you have a notion that some things will take longer than others to complete.

So you will provide the 'accepted average', based on the period of time that you have within which to do the research and to write it up. In general, you will have about five to six months at your disposal. The benefit of putting a timeline into your proposal is that you are forced to think about actually doing the research and the hitches and snags that you might encounter along the way.

Write it down

Starting from now, from when you are on the verge of beginning, write it down, all those stray thoughts and insights and speculations and uncertainties. Get yourself a book and jot it down, not for anyone's eyes but your own – or open a folder on your computer where you can put your thoughts. It will save you thinking in circles, which is a natural tendency when you are trying to work out what your viewpoint is.

Back it up

I can't impress upon you fiercely enough that you need to go into paranoid mode and back up everything you do on the computer, and back up the backups. I could tell you horror stories of stolen or lost computers/ laptops, and crashing hard drives that will make your hair stand on end. The protection of your precious work is not a matter for rational actions – go into paranoia overdrive and back it up. When it comes to backing up, you cannot be too careful or too thorough. Believe me, you will be very glad that you have taken my advice.

Ready to begin

There is an English proverb that is irritating because it is true – a stitch in time saves nine. The stitch in time – taking time to think through the things discussed in this and the previous chapters so you know what your own perspective is, what your views are, how you yourself recognise what is real and what is knowable, will save you more than the nine stitches of wasted effort, confusion, mistakes, blind alleys, misunderstandings.

There we have it. You are ready to begin. You know about the kind of researcher you are. You have an idea of how you would prefer to research and you may even have more than an inkling of what it is that you want to research. You have it clear in your mind what your business school has decided a Masters dissertation in management and business is, and you have a number of tips about how to recognise that you can now move from padding about restless and anxious on the outskirts of the research adventure, and you can simply begin.

4 The problem with the research problem

The trouble with the research problem

While English is one of the most flexible of languages with a vast vocabulary, when it comes to research, there is great scope for confusion. And it happens right at the start – you will discover that whatever it is you want to find out about is called a number of things. It is a research problem, research question, research statement, research topic, research study. Often, however, the area or issue being researched is not a problem at all, but rather a troublesome challenge that needs to be tackled and overcome. Sometimes the research question is just that, a question that exercises the mind, something proposed for academic discussion and answer. But then, you will find that a research question is expressed as a statement, not a question, pointing out a problem or puzzle or mystery that needs to be resolved, something which is a source of perplexity, distress, or vexation, a matter of inquiry, discussion, or thought.

That is why statements like 'The effects on business practice of the growth of corporate social responsibility', or problems like 'Issues of customer retention in financial services' or 'The effect of executive stress on managerial efficiency', or questions like 'How much of a role does motivation and leadership play in the success of an owner-managed business?', or puzzles like 'Does applying business ethics add value within the catering industry?' are all research problems.

From this point on, I use the term 'research problem' and that includes all the other synonyms that tend to be used – research question, research statement, research topic, research study.

Preliminary thoughts

You will find that you have done yourself a good turn if you begin to think about a research problem either while you are doing the taught modules of your course or while the assessed research methods module is being studied. This is an important simultaneous activity that will help you towards success.

Some down-to-earth considerations

It is likely that the most difficult part of your dissertation is finding something to research. Obviously, once you have a research problem, it is a matter of learning how to move forward from that. And because of the difficulty, you may well find that your research methods textbook tends to skate over the surface of the finding the research problem area.

Some students have their research topic imposed on them. If you are being sponsored by your firm, it may be that your employer particularly wishes you to investigate something relevant to the firm's needs.

Another difficulty is that the topic that interests you most cannot be researched in the time available for the production of the dissertation. Or you may find that you don't have the funds to travel to undertake sufficient interviews or pay the postage on enough questionnaires.

In an ideal world, your supervisor will be interested in your topic and be pleased to supervise you. Indeed, sometimes a tutor will mention a topic he or she is interested in, but doesn't have time to research. It would benefit both of you if you were willing to undertake it, supervised by the tutor. But it is possible that you are just one of the number of students that the supervisor is obliged to take on, and he or she may lack interest in your topic or competence to supervise it. You may find yourself being nudged towards making adjustments to your topic so that the supervisor is more engaged in the supervisory process. This is an uncomfortable situation for you both to be in, and sometimes nothing can be done about it other than just to grit your teeth and get on with it.

Most research methods textbooks emphasise the importance of defining clearly the research topic as a problem to be solved or a question to be answered. This should be the starting point for research, rather than the techniques that are going to be used.

The problem with the research problem, however, is that it takes time to find a good idea and more time to refine it into a workable research problem, and often you don't have enough time. When your research methods course begins, you will be told that there is an assessment at the end of it, and the assessment is to take the form of a research proposal. Unless you start thinking about what you might wish to research from the beginning of the course, you may find that you end up with just the period between the end of the course and the deadline for handing in the proposal, which is often not long enough to settle on a good idea.

Deciding on your research problem

There is no foolproof and automatic way of generating research questions. Your research methods book, if it deals with this issue, is likely to suggest you employ the logical sequence of first deciding on a general research focus, and then refining that down to one or two specific questions.

Depending on the type of researcher you are, you will find it comfortable to do what the research methods textbooks suggest and move from a general research area to a specific research problem, or you will prefer to have a specific question or statement in mind, and you will then look for a context for it and a research area in which to situate it. Like everything else to do with research, there is no one best way, which is why it is so important to know yourself as a researcher.

The main reason why there are so many ways to generate or discover your innovative or interesting research question is that the selection of it is not just a single act or simple decision on your part. It is a process that is the end result of your way of thinking, your attitudes, your interests and your degree of motivation. You will approach your research with a mixture of personal experience, theoretical or ideological convictions, direct or indirect involvement, and knowledge. Nobody plucks a research problem out of the air with total and unique creativity or originality.

Some helpful guidelines on what to look for

The first thing, and often the most difficult thing of all, is to find a gap in knowledge or an unresolved controversy or an unanswered question to research. You will need an awareness of current issues in the subject, and although there are uncounted questions and unresolved problems that interest you, not every one of them is a suitable subject for your dissertation.

- **The topic needs to be of great interest to you because you will be spending many months investigating it. If your intellect and emotions aren't engaged, you are going to find it difficult to motivate yourself, when there are so many other more interesting things to do rather than your research.**

- This is a difficult one, but makes sense – the point of asking a question is to find an answer, so the problem you select should be one to which you can offer a solution or answer or explanation. Your supervisor's experience should be helpful here, and it would benefit you to have a preliminary discussion about the potential topic before you begin to plan researching it.

- Then there is the fact that you need to choose a topic that can be researched in the time available to you to undertake the study. You can cover a wide field only superficially, so the more you restrict the area of study, the more detailed it can be.

- This leads on to the observation that if the problem is trivial or superficial, then it isn't worth the time and effort you will be putting into investigating it. All you and your examiners will be left with is the 'so now I know that, so what?' question which doesn't lead to success.

- Bear in mind that you may have problems of access or difficulties in obtaining the information you need. You cannot carry out research without access to the necessary people or documents, and so you should ensure that you have the cooperation of organisations or individuals essential to your research. No permission to enter, no research possible, no matter how carefully planned in advance it has been.

- And, there is the matter of cost – a topic may require travel or postage or other expenses which you cannot cover.

- Watch out for over-enthusiasm. There is little purpose in deciding on a dissertation topic that involves and stimulates you and about which you are motivated and enthusiastic, if it isn't feasible and cannot be accomplished in the time available to you.

One of the 'tests' that will help you to know that you have found a suitable topic is being able to provide a single sentence, understandable by anyone, clearly explaining what the topic of your research is.

What you need to know

To find, or form a research question that is viable, feasible and interesting, you will need to be familiar with the area into which your intended research will fit. This will enable you to have the confidence to speculate on ways in which to develop, extend or clarify aspects of the field.

You will also need to know whether or not you are reinventing the wheel. It is one thing to replicate another person's research, for instance to confirm or rebut the fact that the finding(s) still hold, and quite another to undertake research that has already been satisfactorily dealt with by somebody else, but you haven't looked carefully enough at the literature to be aware of this.

Your search for a research topic is going to be affected not only by your own inclinations, but by the requirements of the business school and, often, of your employer.

Broadly speaking, you are likely to be one of the two kinds of dissertation student – the under-focused or the over-focused. If you are under-focused, your ideas of a subject area are not specific enough to form the basis of a viable topic, and if you are over-focused, you have the single-minded aim of undertaking a specific topic and no other.

The under-focused student needs help to focus generalised and possibly vague thoughts about a research topic. You will need some means to identify a researchable opening that you are capable of using in the time you have available to you. If you are over-focused, you may find that the topic you insist on researching has either already been researched, or that you don't have sufficient time to do the topic justice. Sometimes, the best decision the over-focused student can come to about the topic, is to drop it, and move to something more feasible, if less interesting or exciting.

Check out your own position – want to or ought to?

Your basic problem with your research problem is going to be something that may well be your best kept secret – whether you want to do the research, or whether you are going through the motions because you know you ought to do it, if you want your qualification. Only you will know whether you are a 'want to' or an 'ought to' researcher, though it is likely that your supervisor will guess.

The key to successful research of any kind is that the researcher wants to undertake the research and is genuinely curious about the results. The 'want to' researchers win hands down because they are not swimming against the tide, but are going with the flow. They don't have to flog themselves to sit down and do a bit more on the dissertation. They may be finding it difficult and frustrating, but they have the motivation to presevere through the dark patches because they are interested in the eventual outcome.

'Ought to' researchers, who are doing the dissertation because it is part of their Masters programme, are their own worst enemy. They are constantly fighting themselves, and forcing themselves to get on with what they are finding a boring chore for a qualification rather than an exciting adventure into knowledge.

I must confess that I don't know how to convert the joyless 'ought to' student into a 'want to' researcher. It is one of those things that you have to do for yourself.

Initial explorations

The topic search can be undertaken in four logical steps:

- **find what interests you in a broad subject area**

- **narrow the interest to a feasible topic**

- **examine the topic from several points of view**

- **support your project with a clear rationale.**

The truth of the matter is that, mostly, finding a topic doesn't happen that way. What actually tends to happen is that once you have decided on the broad subject area, you will need to do some reading in order to narrow things down to something you can undertake in the time available. Often, during this process, you read something tangential or peripheral to the broad topic, and this interests you enough to lead you to have a closer look at it. It wouldn't be unusual to start out looking at absenteeism, find that sometimes people don't go into work because they are being bullied, and so end up doing a dissertation on harassment at work.

The reading around will help you to discover what has already been written about your potential subject, what research has been carried out, what further work needs to be done, and what issues still remain.

Thinking about research aims

Start at the top, so to speak. Choose from the three overarching aims of research.

Problem solving

 The way in is to identify a 'real life' problem, with the aim of finding possible solutions by using the techniques of research, which provide a systematic appraisal, analysis and evaluation.

Practical benefits are likely to result from undertaking the research, though sometimes solutions may not be obvious or clear-cut.

Testing-out

 Testing-out research aims to explore the validity of generalisations in specific circumstances, and to define their limits. This is achieved by the researcher examining specific instances in order to test out old generalisations or to make new generalisations from specific instances.

Exploratory

 This kind of research tends to tackle new problems on which little or no previous research has been done. This leaves the researcher free to define the scope of the research, with the hope that the result will be an extension of existing knowledge.

Which route to choose? The one that is safest for you, your temperament, your skills and your experience. Probably it is testing-out research, because it is based on known theories and established methods of testing. This is not to say that you can rely on not encountering any surprises, if you take on this research aim. And you will still have to provide something new – a new insight or a new method or a new viewpoint to make the research more than a replication of what has already been done.

It therefore depends on your own attitude to risk and your capacity to bear the anxiety of the unknown. As long as you are sure of your abilities and have the support of your supervisor, taking the less safe option might provide you with an enriched research experience.

Sources of ideas/topics for a research problem

You are one of a long line of students who has undertaken a dissertation at your institution. Your predecessors' work will be in the university library. Go and have a look at these dissertations, especially those in the area that interests you. You may get ideas for your own research problem, or ideas about how to tackle the work, and you will certainly get a notion about what is an acceptable standard of work in your business school.

Topics are not copyright. Copying someone else's work on a topic is a breach of copyright. Universities are becoming ever stricter about plagiarism, and you absolutely need to know exactly what your institution considers to be plagiarism so that you avoid those practices. The worst case scenario for a plagiarist is to be failed. The last thing you want, after all those months of work, is to be failed for plagiarism.

The reality of finding the research problem

Be prepared for false starts and finding that you have gone up a blind alley and have to turn back and start again. If nothing lights your fire, it will be helpful to look at past dissertations, or search for ideas and themes in journal papers. Most tutors will be willing to discuss embryo ideas with you, and your fellow students are likely to have interesting or helpful opinions.

Most likely, however, you will use one of the two main methods – either logical, rational thinking or intuitive means.

Logical thinking to find your research problem

When it comes to logical thinking techniques, a good guide is your own assessment record. The marks you have been given for your assessed work are a very clear indication of your areas of strength, and indirectly, perhaps, your main areas of interest. It is common sense that if you are interested in something, you are more likely to want to put in the effort that will result in a successful dissertation. Looking logically at past projects in the general area that you are interested in could reveal unproved assertions, areas of confusion, or gaps in research.

Other sources of your research problem could be practitioners, professional groups, or even colleagues at your current (if you are part-time) or former (if you are full-time) place of work. In addition, some research methods books list project ideas in their appendices. Ideas are not copyright so you are free to adopt and adapt ideas from such lists.

Intuitive ways to find your research problem

Your awareness of the kind of researcher you are and the kind of research you would enjoy doing is a good starting point. If you look at past projects or published papers, you could compile a list of the things that appeal to you about these projects – and, perhaps even more importantly, the things that you dislike.

What using your intuition could provide is access to your subconscious attitudes, so trusting your feelings can be as valid as intellectualising your choice of research problem. Ideas could well arise from conversations or more formal brainstorming with colleagues. What could well be helpful is to jot down ideas in a notebook as they arise, which will prevent you from forgetting them in the press of present events.

Logic plus intuition

The search for a research problem isn't necessarily either logical thinking or intuitive means. It could be both. The most important thing is that your emotions are as engaged in the project as your intellect. And also that you realise that success in finding an idea that you wish to research is the beginning of a longer process. You will need to refine the idea into a research problem.

Turning an idea into a research problem

The existing literature on your research idea is a valuable resource for turning your idea into your research problem. In consulting the literature, you are doing two things at once. You are using it to refine your idea while, at the same time, you are preparing for the literature review that you will be obliged to write. Almost without meaning to, you will be focusing your literature search. What is helpful at this point is that you are not confined to academic publications, but can be reading around in trade or professional journals, or newspapers and magazines, all of which can trigger an idea or a research problem, or simply provide insights that reveal to you what you want to research or even how to do so. What is important is that you don't confuse potential solutions with the problem.

The method simplified

In the end, it is a matter of narrowing things down. Starting with your research idea, classify it into its broad area, then into its field, and finally its main aspect or aspects. What you are doing is providing yourself with an increasingly more detailed description of the research idea until it has become the research problem. For instance, say that your idea is that you would be interested in looking at the way people are treated at work. The area, then, is likely to be human resource management. If at this point you have a look at some of the literature, you might decide that you are interested in the field of human resource planning. A little more reading and discussion with others might indicate to you that the aspect you are most interested in is staff retention.

Attributes of a good research problem

Listing the attributes of a good research problem provides you with a checklist for success. Guided by my own experience over time, aided by the advice gathered from a great number of research methods textbooks, I suggest the following attributes:

1. **For student research projects, it is important that the dissertation fits the specifications set by the examining business school, and particularly that this is at the 'correct' (i.e. expected) level.**

2. **The research problem lies within your own interests, capabilities and area of knowledge.**

3. **It has benefits beyond its benefit to you, the researcher, stimulating your own intellectual growth.**

4. **You are able to accomplish the research within your financial constraints.**

5. **There is expertise available in the area – your supervisor's experience and interests, and the business school's library.**

6. **If you are undertaking the research supported by your place of work, it addresses the organisation's needs, and has practical value and benefits.**

7. **It contains issues that are both linked to theory and grounded in the literature.**

8. **It provides fresh insights and contains ideas of interest to both academics and practitioners.**

9. **It gives you an opportunity to promote your ideas both in your work and/or by means of publication.**

10. **It is achievable in the time available.**

Reminder of where you now are

You are aware of

- **the kind of researcher you are**

- **the overlap of working on the research area and the research proposal during your research methods course**

- **the process of researching**

- **the decisions you need to make and the potential problems ahead.**

Don't underestimate yourself

Although experience or expertise in a subject is not a prerequisite for doing research, it does have an effect on the early stages of the research. Being familiar with the literature and the potential problem areas is obviously helpful. But remember that you are not a blank page – you have interests, experience and expertise to bring to the search for and the decision on the research problem.

And whatever else, you will be looking with fresh eyes at the topic, and may well end up casting new light on it.

5 The problem with the research process

The trouble with the research process

The biggest problem is that you are likely to have been taught that the research process is a linear business, starting at a clearly defined beginning and concluding at an evident end. It's as though the researcher starts on the research journey and goes straight ahead, passing plainly marked signposts till the journey's end is reached. If only that were the case.

The logic is obvious: Define the problem area → Research the broad area → Refine the area to a feasible topic → Define the topic clearly into a research problem → Consider the research problem in terms of concepts, theories and possible methods → Gather data → Analyse data → Produce findings and recommendations. But the actuality is different.

The research process has also been conceptualised as a circle or wheel, and as a spiral. In the circular version, the hub of the wheel is research theory, connected by spokes comprising the topic, the methods, the data, the analysis, and the findings to the rim of the wheel which revolves along the research path. The spiral version adds a cyclical dimension to the linear view of research. The coiled spirals of process encircle the line of research theory, corkscrewing though the statement of the problem, the formulation of research aims, the data collection, analysis and production of findings, which may suggest further research, leading to the

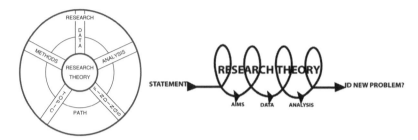

Figure 5.1   The research process

initial identification of a new problem, and initiating a new spiral along the continuing length of research theory. One of the advantages of seeing research as a spiral is that the process is less static, each turn through the spiral repeating the basic process, and the knowledge gained and questions raised at each spiral turn providing the basis for the next cycle.

If research were a logical, objective linear process, you wouldn't need this book. While researching is not always easy or without problems or snags, if it were one-clear-process-after-another, it would be an uncomplicated, straightforward undertaking.

If only it was a linear procedure, as simple as 1,2,3. All you would have to do would be to:

1. **Decide what to do (decide your topic, define your objectives, choose your methodology and methods, obtain willing information sources).**

2. **Do it (collect your data and analyse them).**

3. **Communicate what you have done (develop conclusions, develop recommendations, write dissertation).**

Planning helps

This is not to say that planning is unimportant. It can, and often will, reduce the risk and uncertainty that is part and parcel of research. The advantage of planning is that it:

- **reduces the risk of overlooking or missing something important**

- **helps you to realise when and where you might run into difficulties**

- **will reveal to you where your various activities inter-relate or even overlap**

- **can show you whether your research aims are feasible and can be accomplished in the time that you have available**

- **introduces you to the possibility of creating achievable targets and milestones throughout your research process. You can be more confident of reaching the end of your researching if you find that you are reaching intermediate landmarks on the way.**

If only there were One Best Way to research, so much of the confusion and frustration about planning it, doing it, and writing it up would disappear. But what would disappear also would be the excitement and the fun and the sense of achievement once it is done.

Simultaneous tasks

Applying the metaphor of dance to researching, then what you are doing is line dancing. This type of dance allows the dancer both to dance alone and, simultaneously, to dance in a group. While you are doing your own thing, doing the fixed moves of the dance, you are also part of the group, the line, moving in synch with the other dancers, all of whom are also dancing individually, not touching or interacting with anyone else. Like the line dance, researching for your dissertation is both simultaneous and iterative – you and your fellow students all do the same thing at the same time, separately and yet together, and you repeat the steps through the fixed pattern of the dance.

It is evident that the research process is more a matter of juggling balls in the air than following a logical route. A great deal of the time, you will be doing more than just one thing – you will be reading the literature while drafting your proposal, or learning how to run a computer analysis program while interviewing respondents.

At the basic level, while you are thinking things out, deciding on and discarding various ideas and approaches, at the same time, you could – and indeed, should – be writing these down. This will save you from circular thinking, or thinking the same things over and over again, and, of course, it will prevent thoughts passing through your mind and disappearing from memory. Without noticing it, because you are doing other things at the same time, you will be teaching yourself to undertake academic writing.

Also, at the same time, you could be talking about your ideas to fellow students, tutors, potential supervisors, work colleagues, friends and relatives. These conversations could stimulate new ideas or help you to clarify your current ideas.

While you are conducting your literature search, you should simultaneously be making notes on what you are finding, and beginning the rudiments of what will turn out to be your literature review and items for your research proposal, and reading up on research techniques. It is all very well to decide that you will do your data gathering by means of interviews, but you need to know about how to interview, and what to do with your interview recordings or notes. And that means reading research technique books and books about analysing data at the same time as you are deciding on which techniques are likely to be the most appropriate for your research.

This leads on to another simultaneous activity. When you are planning your questionnaire or interview schedule, you need, at the same time, to be building in aids to analysis. If it is a questionnaire, you will need to code it, because you will be putting the questions/statements into a computer program for analysis. Interview transcripts also need to be in a format that will allow you to easily upload them into a computer program. The requirements of analysis or interpretation should be at the back of your mind all the time you are creating your data collection tool.

You will probably find further activities, specific to your own research, that could, and perhaps should be carried out at the same time. There is, after all, no reason to proceed using the ideal/idealised linear method of doing one research activity after another, just because this is the method strongly advocated by your research methods textbook or your research methods classes.

I have included further comments about simultaneous activities in the Time Schedule section below.

Iteration

Then there are the things that you have to return to, and do again, improve or add to, or remove, or shorten. Two prime examples are your proposal and your literature review.

Your proposal is your entrance ticket to the performance of your research. It will have been written in the future tense, listing what you intend or propose to do. It is a kind of prophesy or prediction of what will happen in the future. But your proposal is also a section of your dissertation, only now it is relabelled as 'research design', and it reports what you have done in order to accomplish the research. So you need to revisit the proposal and change it into a report – for example, from 'the data will be collected from people aged over 60 still in employment' to 'the data was collected from people aged over 60 still in employment'.

Even though it is only a matter of months between beginning your research to writing it up, further articles will have been published on the topic. You are going to have to read them, decide how relevant they are, and, if necessary, return to your literature review to include them. Some of the ideas in those publications might have resonance for you, and you might well need to return to other aspects of your research to find a way to include them. This return to the literature should be a continuous, if intermittent, procedure, and while you won't fail if you don't keep up with relevant publications, you also won't turn your adequate pass into a possible distinction.

Most importantly, iteration is the foundation of your data analysis. You need to know your data thoroughly so that you employ analysis procedures that are relevant and likely to produce of meaningful information. With interviews, it is a matter of common sense to read and reread the transcripts. With questionnaires, it will be a matter of revisiting the variables. Even the simplest comparison and contrasting of percentages will provide you with a sense of which are likely to be more important or more informative than others, and thus worthy of further tests.

And, of course, you need to iterate your writing. Each time you return to something you have written, it is possible to improve or clarify what you have said, or to question whether it is in the right place in the flow of your 'story'. It is sensible to go back over it until it is easy to follow and reads well. Academic writing is not necessarily something that comes naturally, and reiteration will contribute to improvements in your writing skills.

Expect a rough ride

If you find that things aren't going well, or if disastrous things happen – for instance, at the last moment you are refused access – bite the bullet, take your courage in both hands, and either abandon the data that you have collected or, even more radically, cut your losses and change direction and start again.

Accept that the research process is messy and confusing, that a great deal of the time you will feel you are lost in a fog that only disperses briefly and occasionally, and that the process offered to you in textbooks is an idealised version of the untidy reality.

Accept also that most of the time you will feel anxious or frustrated, but that if you are both intellectually and emotionally engaged in what you are doing, you will also feel a very special kind of excitement and pleasure when things are going smoothly.

Findings reflect aims

An element of the research process that is often skated over is the necessity for the interpretation of the findings to be consistent with the analysis. There must be a clear logical path from the aims of the research, to the original concept or model, to the evidence which has been gathered, to the analysis of that evidence, to the findings.

Because the aims of the research and the findings are closely connected, unexpected findings can put a spanner in the works. If the unexpected findings strengthen your aims, you are well away. But if they seem to negate or weaken then you have a choice to make. The easiest choice is to change the aims so that the unexpected findings are turned into intentional findings. What is more honourable is to incorporate the unexpected findings into your 'story', particularly if they undermine the value of what you expected to find.

In a business and management dissertation, there is always going to be the question (implicit or explicit) 'are the findings useful?'

Research process problems

Research process problems that do directly affect you, however, are those arising from unresearchable questions. Not all management questions are researchable, and not all research questions are answerable. To be researchable, a question must be one for which data collection can provide the answer. Many questions – for example those concerning matters of value or policy – cannot be answered on the basis of information alone. And even if a question can be answered by facts alone, it might not be researchable because currently accepted and tested procedures or techniques are inadequate, and you are not sufficiently experienced to create new procedures which may be appropriate. Sorting out whether or not a question is researchable or not is something which your supervisor can give guidance about, but which ultimately is a matter for you to decide.

Another thing that will create difficulties for your research process is the fact that some types of problems are so complex or complicated, value-laden and bound by various constraints that they aren't open to traditional forms of analysis. It may be that the question has too many inter-related aspects for you to be able to measure or even interpret accurately. The solution to this kind of situation – an exploratory study to provide the information that will allow you to decide whether or not the problem is researchable – is one which you don't have the time for.

Time schedule

You will probably be asked to provide a time schedule with your proposal. It is the most annoying thing to do because it is going to be based on guesswork and supposition. But it is also your initial lesson about the research process.

Two things you need to know about your timeframe:

1. **Everything, simply everything, will take longer than you have estimated.**

2. **You will not have left enough slack to cope with the unexpected.**

Still, if half a loaf is better than none, then an inaccurate timeframe is vastly better than none. The thing is, however, that your timeframe is, of necessity, likely to be linear, while your research won't be. A thought-out and convincing timeframe will, however, be a comfort to your supervisor who will feel that you have the research process under control.

Build in time to step back and re-evaluate your ideas, which will come in useful during those patches when you feel you are making no progress.

One way to create a time schedule that reflects the reality of your research process is to be very instrumental. Break your dissertation down into sections and sub-sections. Estimate the number of pages you will need to deal with each section and sub-section. Estimate times by task and estimate duration times. And don't forget to estimate the time needed to document your research. The standard estimate is four hours per each 1.5-spaced, word-processed page of the final version. What is often forgotten is that the references and bibliography are very time-consuming to set up and check, and you could well use a 6-hour estimate per page.

This method is based on the idea that you will calculate realistic time estimates if you break down your activities into smaller tasks and then combine these estimates. You are likely to find that there are activities that seem impossible to put a time on, but you should make a stab at it because it is better to have a weak estimate than none at all.

Bear in mind that time scheduling can become its own displacement activity, and turn into time wasting. Creating highly elaborate charts in many colours could be a way of putting off starting the research. You need some minimum amount of planning, but don't frighten yourself or get bogged down by making what could be a functional document into an intricate work of art.

Non-linear time schedule

You may find it useful to abandon the customary format of a time schedule, and present it to yourself in non-linear terms. Instead of a flow diagram of first one task and then, when that is completed, another task, create a diagram that links the activities that can be done simultaneously, and those which need iterations. This does not prevent you from entering your estimations of how long it will take you to do things, and it may well provide you with a far more realistic plan for undertaking your research.

Then use your judgement. If it seems to you that the person who is going to assess your proposal would prefer the linear version of your time schedule, there is nothing to stop you from producing this. Set your own simultaneous-iterative time schedule aside briefly, and when your proposal has been accepted, you will be able to use it to guide your research activities.

Don't leave things to the last minute

The first common mistake you are likely to make is so obvious that it almost doesn't need mentioning – leaving things to the last minute. I know that I can shout it out till I am red in the face, and you are likely to ignore this advice. I know that you know all the excuses, because you are attempting to kid yourself as well as your supervisor. A small collection of these self-delusions is that you are going through a bad patch, things aren't progressing, it seems such a monumental waste of time, there are more interesting things to spend time on, you aren't up to it. You can intend all the good things, that you will plan ahead, you will build in extra time for contingencies, you will work so many hours daily, and somehow time just flows away, and there you are, at nearly the last minute, scrambling to complete. There is a limit to the degree of sympathy you will get from your supervisor for not meeting deadlines and accumulating a huge time deficit. Don't antagonise him or her, and the thing that is likely to antagonise your supervisor the most is leaving things to the last minute.

Watch your style

Please don't

- **waffle – it is not your examiner's job to disentangle what you meant to say from what you have said**

- **pad – your examiner knows enough to recognise when you are putting stuff in to impress or increase your word count**

- **be ambiguous or vague – your examiner will spot this and will assume that there is a gap in your knowledge that ought not to be there**

- **simplify – your examiner knows the area, if not the topic. You are writing for a fellow researcher, so there is no need to pitch your work to the level of the understanding of an A-level student.**

- **use any words whose meaning you are unsure of – just because they sound impressive or academic. The quickest way to have your cover blown is to use an academic word inappropriately.**

- **try to be funny or witty – 'inappropriate' is the kindest thing that can be said about this type of approach.**

Envisioning the dissertation as a whole

Once you have embarked on the research journey, it becomes difficult to envision the dissertation as a whole. One thing to bear in mind from the outset is that it is very easy to find, as the saying has it, that you can't see the wood for the trees. Once you are immersed in the research process, you might find that you have lost sight of your ultimate goal, which is to produce a dissertation that you are proud of having done, that will do you credit, and that will give you the qualification you are aiming for.

It is a natural condition of researching that you will have phases of wondering what your research is about, and what contribution your dissertation will make. My advice is that you shouldn't forget that you have a natural aptitude for research. You might lack specific skills, but you have been finding things out (and research is only a very formalised way of doing this) all your life.

It is quite acceptable to push your anxieties to the back of your mind and to concentrate on the process. Just expect those patches of gloom, when you are convinced that you are wasting your time and that, as the saying goes, the game isn't worth the candle. Optimism will return, and the motivation to push on to the end, even when the end seems to be receding as you approach it.

And don't forget, even at the bleakest times, that the research process for business and management Masters is the result of the struggles of your student researcher predecessors, and while it isn't perfect, if you follow the process conscientiously, it is the road that will lead to your success.

6 Time well spent

The research design

What actually is a research design?

Put simply, your research design is the plan or overall scheme of your investigation, designed to provide you with the answers to your research question.

The research design provides and accomplishes a number of things. It:

- **is always based on the research question**

- **guides the selection of sources and types of information required**

- **is the framework that enables the specification of relationships among the research's various aspects**

- **makes available the procedures for every research activity to be undertaken.**

The research record and diary

Designing and carrying out research is a chaotic activity, undertaken in lurches and stumbles. One of the ways to help maintain your equilibrium is to keep a research record.

Keeping a record of your research is an effective way to keep control of what you are doing, and the information you deal with. It doesn't really matter what you keep it in – a ring binder, a dedicated notebook, a box file, or even just a cardboard box. The basis of good project management is the keeping of accurate, consistent and correct records.

It doesn't matter what you put in it; after all, the point of the whole thing is that it is there to help you through your research process. Your research record will come into its own when you are doing your literature search. It is somewhere to keep the notes you have made on what items have been ordered and/or obtained through inter-library loan or from your business school's library. It will help you keep track of the literature, reminding you of what you have already got and what needs to be followed up.

You've been advised to have a time schedule, and keeping weekly or monthly plans in your research record helps you to keep track of what needs to be done, read, or written. It is very satisfying to tick off the tasks as they are done, and shows the progress you are making.

You can keep your research record as an objective log of your actions while carrying out the research. But what might well be even more helpful is to convert it into a research diary.

It can be very satisfying to have a private place to conduct a conversation with yourself, to put down your ideas so that they don't get forgotten, to make comments about what you are doing and your feelings about the whole dissertation process, to have a private space to rant and rave when things aren't going well, and to pat yourself on the back when you have achieved a success, and to celebrate when something good has happened.

In an ideal world, you could have a colleague on your course with whom you can share all aspects of the ups and downs of your parallel research processes, but even if you do have a research companion to support and encourage you, there is always something that can't be expressed, and the research record and diary comes up trumps.

Aims and objectives

Check whether you are expected to provide the purpose of your research in terms of aims, or aims and objectives. Aims are intended to provide a broad indication of the purpose of the research. When aims are subdivided, they become objectives – more precise statements of intent, often describing the actual activities which the researcher intends to undertake. It isn't necessary to break down your aims into objectives unless either you or your business school prefer this mode. When you provide your aims, use verbs – you are, after all, stating what the research intends to do. The verbs that tend to be used to express research aims are, for example, to:

- analyse
- discuss
- examine
- explore

- investigate
- propose
- synthesize
- test

Significance of your research

'Significance' is a very daunting word to apply to your own research, but it is something that you need not merely to bear in mind, but to be conscious of. It is probably easier to view the significance of your research in terms of the contribution you are making to knowledge, however modest that may be. And you *are* contributing to the available literature concerning your topic and you may well have results which are of interest to some aspect of business or management, or to businesspeople or managers.

Your population

One of the ways to avoid all the problems that can beset you when you are dealing with sampling is to use the population. The population is the total collection of whatever it is that you wish to examine. It can be very small (the number of people living in your home) or absolutely huge (all the human beings alive last week).

If you can manage to use the population, you are well away, because sampling issues become irrelevant. Investigating the population – the sales department of your company, the suppliers of raw materials to your firm, the users of one of the services provided by your organisation who access the service in person – is called undertaking a census, which is an easy term to remember because of the census of every member of the UK population that takes place every ten years, which is planned to leave nobody out.

Sampling the population

If the population is far too large to examine, then you are going to have to sample. The basic idea of sampling is that by selecting some of the elements in a population, we are able to draw conclusions about the entire population. The advantages of sampling are:

- the obvious one: that you can actually undertake the research because it is manageable

- the likelihood that it will cost less to sample than to do a census – why ask all 2,000 people who work for your organisation when you can reliably get what you need to know by asking a few hundred (although they need to be the correct few hundred)?

- the possibility of greater accuracy – there are times when you can be more thorough when you have fewer things or people to test or ask or observe

- the likelihood of better processing of the information obtained, if only because there is less of it

- the greater speed of data collection, because it is being collected from fewer sources.

There are times when you simply have to sample – testing the resistance to heat of some material may necessitate destroying it. What would be the point of doing a census and destroying all of that material in order to find out the point at which it catches fire?

But bear in mind that when the population is small enough, and the variability within the population is high, then a census is the better choice than sampling. That's because when the population is small and variable, it is difficult to choose a sample that is representative of the population you have drawn it from.

The importance of getting the sampling right

If your sample isn't right, your research is going to be threatened, and more importantly, your findings are going to be suspect. And if your findings are queried, and disbelieved, then all that effort you have put into your dissertation is wasted.

So pay attention to what your research textbook says about sampling, and consult your supervisor to be really sure that your sample is representative and will lead you to valid and reliable results.

The research 'body'

Your research is intended to contribute to what is sometimes called a 'body of knowledge'. If you imagine that this 'body' is not an abstraction but a human body, then your research design, whether in the form of a research proposal or a research design chapter in the dissertation, is the spinal column, the backbone upon which everything else depends. The research design spine supports everything else. It will make clear to you:

- **how you intend to answer your research question, deal with your research problem or solve your research puzzle**

- **that what you want to do is feasible, and that it can be done in the time available**

- **what your specific aims and objectives are**

- **that you can get access to the data that will enable you to meet your research aims and objectives**

- **any ethical issues so you can act to avoid causing harm to yourself and to others**

- **how you intend to get hold of the information you need**

- **how you can analyse the information you have gathered so that you can meet your aims and objectives.**

Research procedure

Try out the various things you could do during the research process in your head/imagination, and talk about it with your colleagues. Their comments and opinions could be helpful – either by allowing you to confirm for yourself that what you plan to do is feasible and possible, or by creating doubts that prompt you to rethink things so that you are confident that you are doing the right thing before you commit yourself to action.

Your timeline – yet again

The thing always to bear in mind is that your research isn't a matter of doing-one-thing-after-another but of doing-all-sorts-of-things-at-the-same-time. Nevertheless, the more detailed your timeline is, the clearer the process of what you are undertaking will be to you. Remember that this is the real timeline for your own use, not the timeline that you produce for the research proposal that only needs to seem feasible in the time allowed.

Activity		Estimated duration in days	Date to undertake activity
Write down concepts and theories of relevance obtained from the literature in order to include them in the data collection instrument(s)			
Select sample			
Find out about possibilities for access			
If using a questionnaire: obtain statistical skills If using interviews: obtain interviewing skills	Attend training course on use of computer package for data input and analysis		
Select and approach people willing to pilot questionnaire/interview schedule			
Pilot questionnaire/interview schedule			
Decide how to present the findings and learn how to produce tables, graphs and other graphics			
Correct the final draft and get it to the binders so that it is ready for handing-in on time			
Time for emergencies, crises, illness, job interviews, and other general contingencies			

Try writing it out in a linear fashion first of all, putting it in a table that lists the activity, the time you estimate the activity might take you, and the date when you will undertake it. Then you can bracket the things you will do at the same time, or colour them with the same coloured highlighter pen. For instance, a table of some of the activities you will need to undertake could look like the table on p. 69.

Another way of creating a timeline is to build up what I call on Order of Action network diagram. For instance:

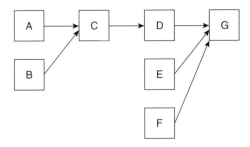

The diagram indicates that:

1. **Actions A and B must be completed before Action C can start.**

2. **Action C must be completed before Actions D, E and F can start.**

3. **Actions D, E and F must be completed before Action G can start.**

The benefits of presenting your timeline in this way is that you can clearly see the inter-relationship between the various activities you need to undertake, particularly when it isn't immediately obvious that some can be done simultaneously, or that one activity has to precede another.

A stitch in time

The proverb 'A stitch in time saves nine' is very irritating because it is true. Taken literally, sewing up a small tear in a garment the moment it is torn saves having a larger sewing job to do if the tear is ignored and grows in length.

When it comes to research design, a stitch in time is very relevant. Taking care to think of as nearly everything as you can, rather than pitching in and hoping things will work out, will save you effort and will prevent mistakes

Your research record and diary will prove to be your accident insurance. Like all accident insurance, the best outcome is to have it, and never need to use it.

7 What they said about your topic

The literature search and review

The researcher as juggler

This is the point where you become a juggler in earnest. You will have at least six balls in the air at the same time – you will simultaneously be:

- **undertaking a literature search**

- **reading the literature your search has turned up**

- **beginning to write the literature review**

- **refining your research problem**

- **constructing your research design**

- **writing your research proposal.**

Sometimes the literature search and review become tedious and seem pointless. You can't see the point of looking for what other people have done and then reading and reviewing it, when all you want to do is get on with your own research. But you might come across some piece of information or idea that sparks you off and leads you to thoughts you might otherwise not have considered.

The purpose of the literature search

You are looking for papers and books that relate to your research topic so that you can:

- **expand your understanding of your research problem/question/ dilemma/topic**

- **look for ways others have addressed and solved problems similar to your own**

- **gather background information on your topic so that you can refine it**

- **identify sources for questions that you might use to solve your research problem or answer your research question.**

While you will be expected to integrate the existing literature relevant to your topic into your research in order to establish the current state of knowledge, the hidden agenda requires you to also establish that not only are you fully aware of the current state of knowledge, but also that you are able to use the literature appropriately in evaluating and synthesising the views of others to support your own investigation.

Your research textbook should tell you how to do a literature search. And your business school's library will set up sessions to demonstrate to you how to undertake such a search online. If literature searching sessions are offered, grab them with both hands. They might be mind-numbing or tedious, but what they won't be is a waste of your time. They will teach you techniques for finding your way through the labyrinth of bibliographic information out there in the electronic databases you will need to consult.

When you get to doing your literature search, the important thing, and often the most frustrating, is to choose the right keywords.

It often seems as though the process has been named incorrectly, and you aren't searching for the relevant literature – instead, you are actually searching for the relevant keywords. The right keyword will unlock stacks of relevant publications for you. But finding the right keyword is often a frustrating business.

For once, the textbooks are accurate when they describe the literature search as a logical and linear process. It is one of the few research activities that really is one thing after another:

1. **Have your dissertation title to hand.**

2. **Consult 'hard copy' publications to identify the key words relevant to your research problem – textbooks (and their references), dictionaries (of management terms, for instance), or even encyclopaedias.**

3. **Apply the keywords by searching both online and in hard copy, through indexes and bibliographies, to identify the publications you think may be relevant.**

4. **Get the publications – and read them to evaluate their usefulness to your research.**

Reading what your search has provided

This is another area where it is taken for granted that you know how to read an academic publication. It isn't an innate ability that you are born with, but a skill that you need to develop – and practice is needed to develop it.

I have included in Appendix 1 an explanation of how to read an academic paper in the hope that you will find this helpful when it comes to actually reading the stuff that your literature search has uncovered. Reading anything involves a number of techniques, some of which you have already picked up without being consciously aware of it, and some of which you have to learn. When you need to read an academic book or paper, you can:

1. **Skim: Skimming a book means looking quickly through it and glancing at the list of contents, headings, introductions of chapters, conclusions and the index. Skimming is quick and it can be an efficient way of becoming familiar with the publication on a superficial level. It is useful as a way of checking whether the publication is relevant or if it has the information that you need.**

2. **Scan: Scanning involves a quick search for something specific – a title or a keyword or a page number. When scanning, you ignore everything except the thing you are looking for. You are scanning, for instance, when you look up a name in a telephone directory, or look in a dictionary for a specific word.**

3. **Read to understand: You need to study the chapter, or passage in detail, in order to absorb the major facts and ideas being expressed. You may need to read the section more than once, and you are likely to need to make notes to summarise what you have read.**

Two other reading techniques aren't relevant for your research reading purposes:

1. **Reading each word: There are times when you need to read every word very carefully – for instance, when you are reading an exam question or following a set of instructions to do something.**

2. **Reading for pleasure: While you may get enjoyment out of some of the academic publications that you read, this is a pale shadow of the enjoyment that comes from reading purely to relax, or for entertainment.**

And don't forget

As much as possible, bear in mind that your literature review – in fact, your whole dissertation – is going to be read by your examiner(s). Try to make what you write as easy to read as possible. Common sense will tell you that something that is a pleasure to read is going to result in higher marks than something which is badly expressed and which needs work to understand.

Evaluating your literature

One of the problems you will encounter once you have completed your literature search is that not all information is of equal value. Judging what is of great and what is of lesser value to you is something that you simply have to learn by trial and error as it can't be formally taught.

Before you begin your literature review, you would do well to evaluate what you have uncovered when searching. There is no point in including iffy information in your literature review; it will only cast a shadow on your own work. Take a tip from librarians who evaluate and select information sources based on five factors that can be applied to any type of source, printed or electronic, and ask yourself questions:

1. **Purpose**
   What is the author trying to accomplish? For instance, broaden knowledge within a field or discipline, or inform non-specialists about some topic in easy-to-access-language?

2. **Scope**
   How much of the topic is covered and in what depth? What were the criteria for inclusion of the information? What time period does the source cover? Is this time period relevant to your research?

3. Authority

   What is the authority of the source – are the author and his or her credentials given? If it is a scholarly article, has it been peer-reviewed? That is, before publication, have colleagues from other universities commented anonymously on the research presented? A great deal of what you will find on the Web will have been published directly, bypassing the peer review process, and may be flawed.

4. Audience

   Who is the publication intended for? It is often difficult to work out who some Web resources are aimed at – and often it is multiple audiences, and not necessarily researchers. Ways of working out who the publication is intended for includes considering the vocabulary used, the types of information provided and the ways in which this information is provided.

5. Format

   How is the information presented? Is it easy to find? How has it been arranged – alphabetically, hierarchically, chronologically? This will affect how easily you can retrieve information. Are there cross-references to similar material? The format of an electronic source will have been designed with the prospective audience in mind, with care being taken to provide links or to cater for people unfamiliar with the Web.

What is a literature review?

There is a lot of fuzziness about what a literature review actually is. The textbooks will tell you that it examines recent or important research studies, company data, or industry reports, and that these publications form the basis for a proposed study. There are two main kinds of literature that you need to review:

1. Conceptual literature: This is written by authorities on the subject you have in mind. It offers opinions, ideas, theories or experiences, and is published in the form of books, papers and articles.

2. Research literature: This gives accounts and results of research which has been undertaken on the subject, and is presented in the form of papers and reports.

The purpose of the literature review

By listing the important publications concerning your topic, you are doing a number of useful things. You are:

- discovering the context in which your research is placed

- uncovering relevant material published in your chosen field of study

- searching for a suitable problem area

- identifying actual questions or statements you might use when undertaking your data collection

- indicating that you are aware of prior research on your topic, and who the big players in the area are

- identifying sources for your own sample frame

- drawing attention to:

    (a) important results and conclusions of other studies

    (b) the relevant data and trends from previous research

    (c) particular methods or research designs that you feel would be helpful – or that should be avoided.

Through the discussion in the review, you are placing your study within the field, and you are pointing out that it will appraise the shortcomings and/or information-gaps in the field.

How to turn the literature search into the literature review

Your supervisor will tell you that what is required from your literature review is not simply a description of what has been published on your topic. He or she will probably get as specific as to say something along the lines of 'Don't just say that Author A says this and Author B says that. You need to review what they have said', which, of course, leaves you no wiser.

What your supervisor means is that you need to evaluate and discuss what you have read in terms of what you are intending to do, pointing out (a) the relevance, (b) strengths, and (c) weaknesses of the publication, both in its own right and for your purposes.

And again and again

The major trouble with your literature review is that it isn't done just the once, and set aside while you complete your dissertation. Once you have your findings, you need to go back to the literature review and see where the connections are. You may have to weed out the bits that are less relevant or even irrelevant to what you have found.

What to do

Your textbook will tell you all the things you need to do when writing your literature review, and most of these are common sense. For example, you will be advised to:

- identify and discuss the relevant key studies on your topic

- include as many up-to-date publications as you can

- take care to be accurate with names, titles and dates

- use extracts and examples to justify your analyses and your argument – and cite them accurately.

What not to do

What is possibly more important, however, is what not to do. Make sure that you don't:

- leave out any important publications on your topic

- discuss central ideas without citing or referencing whose ideas they are

- misspell authors' names or get the titles, dates, pages, or places of publications wrong

- be boring or tedious or pedantic

- believe everything you read and reproduce it uncritically

- give the impression that you are drowning in your information

- try to impress your examiner by using pretentious language or jargon.

8 Getting your information and dealing with it

Doing data

At last, the exciting bit, made more stimulating because you are travelling in two different ways simultaneously. You will be working in a linear way – doing one thing after another – and concurrently, you will be doing a number of other, non-linear activities – for instance, you need to use data collection and analysis techniques at the same time as you are learning how to use them.

The whole data area is the part of researching that I think of as the learning-to-ride-a-bicycle section. Firstly, data collection and analysis and learning to ride a bike share the fact that you need to learn something that cannot be taught. Secondly, they are both situations of 'no-doing = no-learning' and 'learning-while-doing'.

Collecting data

When you think about it, there are only four ways to get the information that you need for your dissertation:

- **Ask**
  You can ask for the information in a number of ways – face-to-face and one-to-one, or face-to-face and in a group, over the

telephone, on the Web, on paper. This is the main method of data collection, because it goes straight to the heart of the matter under investigation.

- **Do**
  You can participate in the activity that you are interested in. This enables you to learn directly what it is like to do it, how much skill is needed to do it, and what doing it can accomplish.

- **Watch**
  You can observe others doing whatever it is and still learn a lot about the activity.

- **Watch and do**
  And, of course, you can do both at the same time – do the thing yourself in the company of others and watch others doing it at the same time.

For academic purposes, these activities (which we all do in our everyday lives) have been given names – asking is called Surveying or Interviewing, doing is called Participation, watching is Observation, and watching and doing is Participant Observation.

Historical data

You are unlikely to come across one of the problems that concerns historical researchers. They work with documents, and have the problem of ascertaining whether or not they are authentic. If you do need to use business documents, such as memos, minutes or reports, they are likely to be genuine and relatively recent.

The other issue that concerns historical researchers also concerns you, and needs some thought and maybe even some further investigation – whether what the documents say is the truth or not.

Data and information

Data are facts, attitudes, behaviour, motivations, and so on, collected from respondents or observations, plus published information relevant to a piece of research. Not all pieces of information are data because not all information is appropriate for your purposes.

Primary data are data that you have collected through direct enquiry, observation, experiment or participation. Secondary data have been collected by others – and you will access these during your literature search, for instance.

Don't confuse primary and secondary data with primary and secondary sources. Primary sources are those documents which, or people who, provide data directly; secondary sources report on what other documents or people have written or said.

Data collection and analysis

There is no point in telling you here how to collect or analyse your data. Your research methods textbook will do so, and your supervisor will add to that information.

It is only necessary to mention that you can either dedicate your time and attention to firstly collecting your data, and then subsequently to analysing it, or you can do a number of other things at the same time – work on your background or contextual chapter(s), learn more about, and practise, analysis techniques in preparation for the completion of the data collection phase(s), create a draft layout for the findings chapter(s).

Presenting your findings

What your research methods textbook may not discuss in any detail is the matter of writing up your results. It is a fact of research life that a quality presentation of research findings can have a very large effect on a reader's (examiner's) perceptions of a study's quality.

Underlying any presentation of findings are two questions:

1. **What does the reader need to know about what has been found in order to accept the validity of the argument?**

2. **What is the best way to present the findings so that they are easily understood?**

The second question, in turn, leads to further questions:

3. **What particular point is being made by the finding?**

4. **What is the meaning or significance of this particular finding?**

5. **How important is it to the argument?**

You are likely to have collected more data than you need or that you can profitably use. Some findings will need to be presented in narrative form – other findings are best provided as tables, graphs or figures. You will need to give thought to which type of finding will benefit from what kind of presentation. For instance, relationships, or patterns of causation or interaction are probably better presented in the form of a diagram, using boxes, arrows and other linkages than in sentences.

You may find that it is sensible to place the most important tables in the main body of the dissertation, and to put other, less important, but equally informative tables in an appendix.

If you are using tables and charts, remember to use the academic method of numbering them – for example, if your findings chapter is chapter 6, then your tables will be presented in sequence numbered Table 6.1,

Table 6.2, Table 6.3, and so on. The same applies to figures, charts and graphs. And give them all a title or heading.

Intelligent use of tables, charts, graphs and diagrams can enhance your presentation of findings, and make them more comprehensible, accessible and attractive.

Computers now make it possible to produce a wide variety of 'pictures' in your write-up to break up the pages of uninterrupted text. And Brown's Law has it that 'when it comes to dissertations nowadays, if it is possible to do something, then it is expected that the something will be done'. And so, you will need to learn about the variety of graphs, charts and diagrams available to you, and to master how to produce bar charts, pie charts, histograms and the sundry other pictorial ways of presenting your findings. (For instance, if your textbook is a good one, it will tell you that when it comes to graphs, you can choose from column, bar, stacked bar, pie, stacked multiple pie, line, filled line, area, scatter, bubble, spider and pictographs.)

There are a number of simple techniques you can use to enhance the presentation of your findings:

- **Use white space and good margins, because this will create a positive impression on your reader.**

- **Break large pieces of text into smaller units with headings that clarify the organisation of the findings.**

- **Emphasise your important findings – careful use of italics or underlining can be helpful.**

It is a sad fact of life that lack of confidence and an inaccurate self-evaluation of what you have achieved can sabotage your good work through inadequate presentation. It is an even sadder fact of life that mediocre findings excellently presented can be more impressive than exciting findings badly presented. Don't let this happen to you.

Designing the discussion of findings

There is something you need to bear in mind when designing your research. Connected to the decisions you need to make about how to present the findings are decisions about discussing them.

There are two main ways of dealing with findings:

1. **You can list them, either in text or graphically, and then, either in a new chapter, or at the end of the listing, you can discuss them.**

2. **You can present a finding, discuss it and then present the next finding, and discuss that.**

It might be sensible to discuss this with your supervisor because he or she, or even the business school's 'house style', may have preferences about how findings should be presented and discussed.

A word of warning

Just as it is counter-productive to design a complicated piece of research that will stretch you to your intellectual and energy limits to accomplish, so it is equally unhelpful to get carried away when it comes to presenting your results. There is simply nothing to be gained by producing an intricate diagram that looks really good, but which says nothing of substance.

Be brave. Despite the effort that it took you to get hold of a particular piece of information, if it adds nothing to the point of the dissertation, bite the bullet and leave it out. Better a few findings of interest than lots of findings that evoke a 'so what?' response.

Thinking of research in the future

In advising you to discover the methods you are temperamentally drawn to, I am possibly planting the seeds of future problems. The possible difficulties don't apply to your dissertation, your first piece of systematic investigation, but should you continue to research, you may find that my advice is counter-productive.

For instance, you can become tied to favourite methods. This will lead you to do exactly what I have advised – to recast your research question so that it is amenable to your preferred methods – and this may result in research driven by inappropriate techniques.

If you discover that you have access to a pool of information already gathered or a database, I suggest that you clap your hands and dive straight in. The more experienced researcher may well be reluctant to gather more information because what he or she already has access to renders making the effort unnecessary. But the risk is that the same database gets recycled again and again, regardless of the fact that time and circumstances have moved on. The information was originally gathered with a specific purpose in mind, and it may not be appropriate for the new research being undertaken.

9 Writing matters

When to start writing

You have, of course, been writing from the beginning. You've been writing down plans of what you want to do and how you might do it, and you've made notes about what you've been reading. And then, you have written your research proposal and submitted it. Once it is accepted, what happens next?

This is the point where you begin writing in earnest. Your proposal is the springboard from which to launch yourself into the real thing. There are, however, two things you could do now that will help:

1. If it wasn't required for the proposal, now is the time to create your timeline of what you will be doing and when. If you have included a timeline in the proposal, have another look at it to ensure that it is as realistic as you can make it. Make sure that you have included the time that doing your background reading will take, and estimates of how long it will take you to negotiate access.

2. Rough out a draft of your introductory chapters – you needn't do more than note down a series of headings. This will prevent you from being overwhelmed by the realisation that you have taken on a large and complicated task and that you have to accomplish it, to the best of your ability, by a certain date.

If you find that your supervisor is reluctant to comment in detail on your work when you talk about it, you are likely to find that he or she is more willing to guide you once there is something in writing to consider.

Some supervisors will suggest, right at the beginning, that you write from the very start. Those who don't mention it when you first meet probably take it for granted that you will be writing from the outset. What you need to bear in mind is that, if you sit and wait till you feel inspired, you might well find that you are waiting in vain.

Writing up strategies

Even if your Masters course hasn't explicitly covered writing, this doesn't mean that writing can't be learned. Writing ability can be developed through practice. The one thing you will have discovered already from reading this book is that writing up your dissertation isn't the last thing that you undertake. You are writing from Day One, whether you are noting down thoughts that occur to you, or taking notes on the publications you are reading, or recording a list of things to do.

Counting the words you have written in a session can either inspire or demoralise you. Word counting is a way of getting a more accurate measure of output. It may lead you to feel that you are, or aren't, doing enough writing. If you have set a rate that is realistic, then achieving that number of words in an hour or a writing session will show you that you are making progress – but progress of a sort. After all, your dissertation is far more than merely the total number of words that make it up. What you need to be doing is building regular writing into your life, and setting a realistic pace can contribute to this.

While setting yourself a target of so-many-words an hour or a writing-session can be counter-productive, for some of you, this kind of target-setting is exactly the supportive framework that you need. In the end, of course, it is the quality of your writing that is far more important than the number of words you have written. The experience of others indicates that fluency will result from regular writing and quality will come through revision of what you have written.

There is no one-right-way of setting about your writing task. There are at least two different approaches to writing up your dissertation, and probably more. One tactic is to collect all the literature references, all the evidence and the analysis, and write the dissertation. With this approach, all the writing is done as a single task at the end of the research process when all the work has been done. In my view, this just-in-time-to-beat-the-deadline method is something that experienced researchers find difficult, let alone novice researchers writing up major academic work for the first time.

The second strategy is far safer and is the one that I strongly recommend to you. This method is to write up the work as it is in progress, and to begin as soon as the research has been started, or even when it is being planned. I feel that this approach makes writing up more manageable.

And, of course, the more accurately you have kept detailed records of the research as you have undertaken it, the easier the writing of the dissertation will be.

Views about writing

The traditional view is that you must first decide what you want to write and then write about it. But there is much to be said for the view that you can use writing to develop your thinking and to help you decide what you want to write. This idea is based on the notion that writing is a mode of learning. It puts into practice what you have learned about academic conventions, and it is evidence that you are exercising the independent thinking necessary for successful research. This is an acknowledgement that writing your dissertation is an integral part of the research process.

Both the think-then-write and the think-while-you-write strategies have their advantages, and on one level, these aren't opposites. After all, even if you think and then write, when you are writing, you are obviously also thinking.

The order of the writing

Just as you haven't begun the research at the beginning and researched in the logical order to the end, so you don't write like that. The first, central thing to do is to get the research proposal written (and approved). It becomes your research design chapter, the detailed recipe of all that will follow.

Your first full draft will be put together from the chapters that you have written over the period of doing the research. The table below is an indication of the difference between the order that tends to be presented in research methods textbooks, and the order that is actually followed by researchers.

Table 9.1   The recommended order and the done thing

Order of the dissertation	Order of writing
Introduction and problem statement	Research design
Literature review/theoretical background	Literature review/theoretical background
Research design	Findings
Findings	Conclusion
Conclusion	Introduction

How to start writing – open writing

Open writing is the term used to describe a technique that will enable you to get something down on paper and to build your confidence in your own writing. It is way of brainstorming in sentences. Your topic could be anything – for instance, your feelings about writing, or aspects of your research, or what you intend to do next. You continue writing for a set, but short, period of time – say, five minutes to begin with. Don't stop to revise, edit, or rephrase or structure. This is private writing with no reader other than you. Writing in sentences helps you to move beyond the fragments of thought in your head and to synthesise your ideas.

Open writing is quite different from the requirement to know what you want to say before then writing it down. But what it does is to introduce you to the flow of writing, and that can increase your fluency, which in turn will improve your confidence, which may well raise the standard of your writing.

The purpose of writing

A way to lessen your anxiety about writing, and to help yourself to do it, is to be clear about what the purpose of writing is for you, beyond the fact that a written dissertation is a requirement for your degree. Writing is more than simply a means of communicating the 'story' of your research. At different times during your research, you are likely to be writing for different purposes. You may initially be writing to learn or to teach yourself about what you are researching. You are writing to explore your research topic, to document it, to report on it, and to persuade an examiner that you have uncovered or discovered something of interest, significance and value.

Stages of the writing process

Writing anything that isn't simply a letter to a friend which can be dashed off and posted without worrying about the style of expression, needs working on, drafting and redrafting until you are sure that it says exactly what you want to say in exactly the way you want to say it. Thus, writing a dissertation will have logical stages:

1. **Identifying what kind of writing you must do – well, you know that you are required to produce the distinctive type called academic writing.**

2. **Organising the information you have gathered into an outline of what you will write – and your proposal has provided you with that.**

3. **Writing a first draft and submitting it to your supervisor to comment on – you will find that your supervisor is reluctant to get your dissertation in assorted sections, separated in time, because it is difficult to discover whether the argument holds up from disconnected snippets.**

4. **Producing a final draft and editing and refining it, checking that the references are accurate, and that your 'story' flows smoothly and convincingly.**

Putting together a first full draft

One way to start writing and keep writing is to write in 'normal' English. This enables you to get your thoughts clear and to easily express what you want to say without feeling pressured to write it 'properly'. Once it is down there, on the computer screen, or on paper, you can turn it into academic-speak. For someone who is new to academic writing, it actually is quicker to do it twice. It is far easier to improve what is written than to struggle with getting it 'right' first time.

You can consider the first draft of a chapter as you-the-person talking to yourself, and the next draft, as you-the-researcher talking to academics. Writing for yourself is termed 'open writing', and is a way for you to develop your ideas and to gain confidence in expressing yourself. Nobody other than you need ever see it. A simple example – for a novice researcher such as yourself, it is quicker and easier to write down 'I asked seven restaurant workers to fill in my questionnaire and to point out the bits they found difficult to understand or to fill in' than to write first go 'The questionnaire was piloted with seven restaurant workers, who provided comment and suggestions on the format and content of the questions, and the general structure and order of the research instrument'.

Comforting advice

Remember, you don't:

- have to get it right first time – there is nothing restricting you from writing something several times until you are satisfied with it

- start at the beginning and go on till you reach the end – you can write in any order that seems useful to you

- think that once it is written down in a certain order, it has to stay that way – you can rearrange the contents as many times as you wish

- worry about getting your style, expression, spelling or grammar right the first time you write something down – you can, and indeed you must, go back and correct it later.

10 The final effort

How much is enough?

Literally 'enough'

Right at the beginning, you will have found out the word limits that your business school has set for a Masters dissertation. If typed in 1.5 line spacing, a dissertation between 10,000 and 20,000 words in length will take up between 75 and 100 pages. It should take around 6 chapters or sections to cover the required information – the introduction, with its statement of the research aims, the literature review, research design providing methodology and methods, the presentation of the findings and their discussion, and the final drawing of the threads of the argument together.

Every computer now has a word count program, so that it is easy to keep an eye on the length. If you find that you have to go over the word limit, one of the ways to disguise this is to choose a smaller font, or to slightly change the margins.

I have heard horror stories from colleagues who have said that when examining a dissertation they stick strictly to the allowed word count, and they read to that word limit, and stop. As the whole point of your dissertation is going to be placed in your concluding chapter, it doesn't bode well for you if your examiner stops reading before reaching it.

It has come to be expected that a dissertation will have a specific structure.

The basic minimum is these five chapters:

1. introduction

2. literature review

3. research design

4. findings

5. conclusions.

Figuratively 'enough'

On a non-literal level, 'enough' is a matter of sufficiency. In this sense, how much is enough is the amount necessary to tell your dissertation 'story' completely, succinctly, and satisfactorily. This 'enough' is independent of word counts and printing fonts and page layouts, and will creep up on you as you proceed, until you can see it clearly, and feel able to stop.

General writing tips

Which person?

One of the issues which will concern you, is whether it is more appropriate to write your dissertation in the first person ('I interviewed 20 estate agents.'), or the third person ('The researcher interviewed 20 estate agents.'), or to use the passive voice ('Twenty estate agents were interviewed.').

The traditional way is to use the third person or the passive voice. Why is this? Way back, when social science research emerged (and business and management is a sub-field of social science), the dominant model was that of the natural sciences like physics and chemistry. These disciplines mainly used quantitative methods and the research was written up from the perspective of an objective, impartial researcher, emotionally distant from the research.

Using expressions like 'a survey was conducted' or 'the analysis confirmed the hypothesis that ...' suggested that the research had been undertaken in a rigorous manner and that decisions about what to do and what the data revealed were precise and clear. The implication is that the researcher followed defined procedures and protocols, and was able to separate personal values from the activity of researching.

When less positivistic research philosophies were developed, and when it was accepted that the totally objective researcher is an ideal rather than a reality, interest moved from numerical analysis of data, to the interpretation of the meaning of the data. The continuous choices needed while undertaking research highlighted the more subjective nature of researching people rather than natural phenomena like light or helium.

Currently, while the third person remains the dominant means of expression, first person accounts are growing in acceptance. You would therefore be wise to find out what the preference of your supervisor and the 'house style' of your business school is, and to do it their way. The most important thing is that you communicate your ideas clearly and accurately, and in the most appropriate manner, so that your dissertation meets your supervisor's requirements.

Referencing

This is the important bit, and the portion of your dissertation that, if inadequate, will fail you. Not only must you reference comprehensively (because non-acknowledgement of sources is viewed as plagiarism), but you must learn to reference properly (according to what your supervisor and business school thinks is proper referencing). There is bound to be a handout from your course leader or in the university's library about setting out references correctly.

The issue here is that, for any examiner, sloppy referencing = sloppy thinking = sloppy researching = sloppy findings = fail. So, if the reference list at the back of your dissertation has information missing, like page numbers or author's initials, it will count against you, no matter how brilliantly you have presented your research findings and the significance of your research.

Presenting findings

You can present your findings in narrative, text paragraphs. But sometimes, if you have 'numbers', you need to present them in 'pictures'. In the main, there are three ways to write up statistics. You can do so in text paragraphs, in tables, and with graphics. Compared with tables, graphs show less information and often only approximate values. But they convey quantitative values and comparisons more easily than tables. There are computer programs that will make it easy to create tables, and the various graphs that might be appropriate. There are a wealth of 'pictures' you can choose from – for example, various kinds of bar charts, pie charts, area charts, 3-D graphics, line graphs, scattergrams, bubble charts, boxplots and pictographs.

Your research methods textbook, or perhaps a book on statistics, will explain which graphic forms are the ones most appropriate to the information you wish to present. Even the most qualitative of research can be presented with tabular or graphic aids. After all, your ultimate aim in including 'pictures' is to make your findings more readily accessible and easy to grasp.

Writing in a second language

What possibly hasn't occurred to you if you are a non-native speaker of English, is that while you may need extra help with your writing, you may have more knowledge of English spelling, grammar and usage than native speakers. Unfortunately, if English is your second language, and if you therefore need more help with writing, it may be that your supervisor doesn't have the time to give you the extra attention and help that you need. Because this is a general problem, it is likely that the university has a course on English for Academic Purposes, and it would benefit you if you could find the time to attend it. You need to be proactive to find out what help is available to you, and to tap into it.

It is generally considered acceptable for you to receive help in getting your writing up to standard. It is possible to have a native English speaker edit your work and ensure that its grammar, punctuation and spelling is correct, and that your 'story' is not being obscured by poor sentence structure or muddled expression.

Matters of technique, language and grammar

It doesn't need mentioning that a dissertation with slipshod grammar and idiosyncratic punctuation is not going to create the impression that you are a conscientious researcher, and that your research can be trusted.

If you know that your grasp of grammar and punctuation is weak, then you really are going to have to make time to brush up on the aspects that are inadequate. The problem is that grammatical rules are actually only conventions, and change over time. For instance, there was a period when to begin a sentence with 'and', 'but', 'because' or 'however' would have been given a Big Black Mark. This rule or convention is no longer a matter for casting the writer into the Pit of Ignorance. And, it seems that a new convention is in the process of creation – just as 'you' is both 'you singular' and 'you plural', so 'their' is becoming both plural and singular in order to avoid the clumsiness of forms like 'he or she' or 'he/she' or 's/he' or 's(he)'.

Another aspect of expression that is now required usage is gender-neutral language. A reception desk could be 'staffed' rather than 'manned', 'manpower' factors could be 'personnel' factors, 'workmen' could be 'workers'. A 'police officer' rather than a 'policeman' or 'policewoman', a 'headteacher' rather than a 'headmaster' or 'headmistress'. There are ways round the problem of using a single gender pronoun – use the plural, so that you have 'Supervisors use their leadership skills in team-building situations' rather than 'The supervisor uses his or her leadership skills'. Another option is to alternate, using 'he' in one sentence or paragraph and 'she' in another, though this can end up somewhat confusing for the reader.

Issues of content

Relevance and rigour

It is taken for granted that these two qualities will be present in your dissertation. On the one hand, this chapter is the wrong place to discuss them, because if your work is not relevant and rigorous at this stage, it is nearly too late. On the other hand, there is still time, and in the closing stages of your writing up, you have a chance to address these attributes.

The trouble is that while relevance and rigour are commonly highlighted by academics when they discuss dissertations, they tend not to be carefully defined. This is probably because there are several difficult issues involved in a proper definition of the concepts. And these difficult issues tend to concern the question of who the main audience for the research is.

Early on in the book, I tried to tactfully warn you that those of you who are required to do your research on a topic of importance to your employing organisation are likely to encounter more problems than those of you who are able to choose your research problem, free of external obligations. I tell my students who need to research a topic required by their organisation that, to all intents and purposes, they will have to write two documents. The first will satisfy the requirements for the Masters degree that is being studied for. Once this is completed, then the second document can be constructed out of the first – it can be less abstract or conceptual, and can be produced in the form of a report that doesn't need strict academic justification for the recommendations made.

The answer to the questions 'at whom is this dissertation aimed?' and 'who is to be the main beneficiary of the findings?' are likely to be different communities. So, when the term 'relevance' is being considered, you need to be clear that for your immediate purposes, it is academic relevance that takes priority.

In an academic context, 'rigour' refers to the strict application of research rules and logic. This means that whatever methods are chosen for the research, their rules have to be complied with. For instance, the sample size and response rates need to be credible and the techniques chosen for analysis need to reflect the research situation. In that sense, 'rigour' means that all the various steps of the research have been carefully applied. The result of this is that the findings are credible and thus acceptable.

The reason why I have placed the discussion of relevance and rigour here and not at the beginning of the book is that part of your final effort is to make sure that you are using the right language so that your examiner is reassured that relevance and rigour are present in your work. In a sense, it's not just what you say, but the way that you say it. Polite attention drawn to the existence of relevance and rigour in your dissertation is likely to be accepted, especially if you add that you have taken care to minimise bias and personal value judgements, although you know that these cannot be entirely excised from your research.

Limitations of the research

You will benefit if you place a section either in your research design chapter or in your final chapter, which admits to the limitations of your research. Reflect on your research and evaluate your dissertation, admit to your weaknesses, the things you omitted, those which if you knew then what you know now, you could have improved upon – all this will be to your credit.

It is easier for an examiner to 'forgive' mistakes freely admitted than to excuse mistakes which he or she suspects that you don't even know you have committed. Owning up to inadequacies and apologising for them up front is therefore a far better procedure than keeping silent and hoping that the examiner won't notice.

Your supervisor's part in your writing

By reading your writing, either in chapters or as full drafts, your supervisor can alert you to those features of your writing that need to be improved. The problem is that because you are unlikely to be your supervisor's only dissertation student, the business school may have rules about how often your supervisor is required to read and provide feedback on your written work. You need to clarify this early on, because it will make a difference to how you approach the task of writing up.

While your supervisor will try to motivate you to start writing and to keep writing throughout your research process, you do have to take responsibility for and ownership of your written work.

Feedback

You will get different types of comments from your supervisor about your writing – and these will prompt different kinds of revision and changes. You might find some of these comments upsetting, but don't lose sight of the fact that your supervisor intends them to be helpful, to cause you to rethink what you are offering your reader and how you are doing it. It is pointless on your part to ask for feedback only to ignore it. If you aren't sure what action to take, then go back and ask your supervisor what he or she meant. But bear in mind that your supervisor is not also your editor. And, indeed, he or she may not have the skills to teach writing on top of the other skills required for supervision.

If you aren't satisfied with the feedback you get, it may be that you haven't made clear to your supervisor the kind of feedback that you need. There is no guarantee that you will get it, but at least you will have clarified to your supervisor and to yourself what it is that you are trying to do.

Revising your drafts

There is no need to tell you that you are going to write the dissertation more than once. Your supervisor will give you feedback on how to improve your chapters or your complete draft, pointing out what is missing and needs to be added, what is unclear, what there is too much of and what needs to be cut.

When do you know it is ready to hand in?

Ah, how long is a piece of string? There is no simple answer to the question of when you know that you have done enough work of sufficient quality to submit your dissertation so that it can be examined and found worthy of the degree you have been working towards.

One answer is that you know your dissertation is ready when it has fulfilled the requirements that were set out for you to follow when you began. Its depth and scope are governed by the time you have been allowed to complete it.

Another is that you will reach the point where you realise that your dissertation is not finished and, indeed, can never be finished. It is always going to be a contribution to an ongoing search for knowledge rather than a completely finished piece of work. You will reach a point when you stop, rather than finish, because you have run out of time or allowed word count, or because you can recognise that what you have done is acceptable for the award of the qualification.

And yet another answer is your dissertation is ready when your supervisor agrees that you have achieved your research objectives.

What your examiner is going to look for is whether the research question has been answered adequately and that the answer to the research question has been given in an accessible and credible way. This is a matter of judgement and, in the end, you have to trust yourself. Recognising that you have mastered your subject, demonstrated knowledge of the research techniques you have used, and that you have researched and written an adequate and competent piece of work, means that your dissertation is ready for you to hand in for examination.

Evaluation of your dissertation

The kind of writing that your examiner is looking for is 'reader-friendly' – one of those concepts difficult to define, but easily understood. Don't forget that your examiner wants to read a piece of work that has engaged with new ideas or new perspectives on old ideas. Your examiner expects to understand your work, without special assistance, and your aim is to present your work well so that your examiner enjoys the experience of reading it.

Your examiner is likely to be looking to see that you have demonstrated that you:

- **understand the nature and purpose of the research**

- **are familiar with the relevant literature**

- have mastered the necessary techniques to undertake the research

- are capable of assessing the meaning and importance of the findings.

What any examiner is after is a sense that your dissertation can stand alone as an account of the work you have done, and it should be coherent, well-written, well-argued and well-presented. The central issue is that your findings and recommendations have been convincingly communicated.

Implicit in comments like 'well-conceptualised', 'well-argued', or 'well-presented' is that elusive something – 'well-written'.

Check your title

Before you submit your dissertation, have a good look at your title. Does it still fit? Is it still an accurate rendition of the essence of your dissertation? If it is, you can prepare the dissertation for submission. If it isn't, then you need to consider what the real, effective title is. Once you have got that, you are ready to submit.

The very last thing

When it is all done, when reading your final chapter has clarified to you what you have really been doing all these long months, then you have one more thing to do.

Get the dissertation bound, bite the bullet and hand it in.

There is only a short while more to worry and fret, and then – congratulations! Enjoy your success – you deserve it.

Appendix 1 How to read a business/ management academic paper

What is an academic paper in business or management?

The flip answer is that it is a pompous, badly written, boring piece of pretentious pontificating, written by one academic in order to impress academic colleagues and to further his or her career.

A more considered answer is that it is an erudite piece of writing which intends to inform those interested in a mainly intellectual, though sometimes practical, problem, puzzle, mystery or debate about new knowledge or new perspectives on old knowledge, and which contributes to the solving of the problem, puzzle or mystery, or furthering of the debate.

Why read academic papers at all?

Because:

- Even if badly written, academic papers are, in the main, interesting and informative – assuming, of course, that you are interested in the topic or area they discuss, and that you find what they say informs your interest and furthers your knowledge.

- You will gain personally in a number of intellectual and emotional ways by having come into contact with attention-grabbing thoughts, views and opinions that you may not yourself have had.

- When you read an academic paper, you are automatically included in the debate of academic colleagues communicating with one another through the medium of print.

Because, as a student:

- You are required to do so, interested or not.

- You are going to be assessed on how widely you have read and how well you have done so.

- You are likely to acquire skills of application and concentration that will benefit you in other areas of your life.

- It can be exciting to have access to bright minds and clever thoughts and to learn something you didn't know before.

How do you know you will find the paper worth reading?

Often you won't know whether a particular paper is worth reading till you are well into the reading of it. What you can find out, before you begin, is whether the paper is appropriate reading for you. You are helped towards this in two ways:

1. There is an Abstract which, according to convention, should tell you what the paper is about, what the author did to deal with the topic under investigation or discussion, how what was discovered was found out, and what the findings mean in the general, or specific, context of things.

2. There are **Keywords** which highlight the main areas being investigated and discussed. These give clues as to the issues important to the author. They are also useful when you are searching for what papers might exist on certain topics or areas.

Reading the paper

Because business and management academic papers are written according to a particular convention, you not only have to know the convention, but you need to know the particular vocabulary used. Often commonplace words are used in non-ordinary, technical ways, and the author takes it for granted that the reader is familiar with these, and so doesn't define them. For instance, take the word 'question'. A research question is not necessarily an interrogative expression. It can be a statement, an investigation, a puzzle or a mystery that exercises the mind, a source of perplexity, distress, or vexation, or even a difficulty in understanding or accepting something.

Knowing the vocabulary associated with your discipline/area/topic is essential, but the conventional layout of an academic paper is a tremendous help (which is probably why the convention was established in the first place, and is maintained today).

The conventional layout of a business/management paper will look like this:

Title, Abstract, Introduction (including statement of research problem/aims), Background to/Context of the Research, Literature Review, Research Design, Findings/Discussion of Findings, Drawing Conclusions.

How to read the Title

The title should give a good indication of what the paper is about. Depending on the journal, it will either be succinct and about eight words long, or it will have a pithy, witty first part and a colon followed by a longer, more explanatory phrase.

How to read the Abstract

The title gives an indication of what the paper is about, but the abstract needs to do more than just indicate (see above). A good abstract will help you to decide whether or not the paper is relevant to your (research) needs, and whether or not you should bother to continue reading.

How to read the Introduction

Because it is mainly meant to draw the reader into the meat of the paper, the introduction is often just a sophisticated signpost for where you are heading. The main purpose of the introduction is to provide an 'are-you-sitting-comfortably?' section. Here the research problem tends to be stated, or the aims of the research will be listed, and often the last paragraph of the section will tell you what is coming up and how this is divided into further sections.

How to read the Background to/Context of section

There may be a background to/context of the research section. Reading it should give you a better grasp of the situation that gave rise to the research, or the place in the 'real world' into which the research problem might fit.

How to read the Literature Review

Sometimes the background/context is subsumed into the literature review, the purpose of which is to tell you what other authors have already said about the topic. The literature review, if well-written, is a critical appraisal of issues and factors, ideas and opinions, and the results of research that others have undertaken in the area of the present research. A good literature review is not just a description of previous work, but appraises, compares and contrasts it with other relevant work, and with the author's. This is the section that will provide you with references that, if followed up, will widen knowledge and stimulate independent thought. It will broaden your knowledge of the area, and will do so in a critical manner so that you have what you need to form your own viewpoint. The author will have taken ideas, opinions or models from the other authors in the review and incorporated these into the research, and the well-written paper will highlight the connections and disconnections between these others and him/herself at the end of the paper.

How to read the Research Design

A good paper will have a section that discusses how the research was undertaken. It is sometimes (inaccurately) called methodology or, more accurately, research design. A good research design section can teach you a great deal about how to research. It could (and some would say that it should) describe both the author's methodology (philosophy of research, views of what knowledge, reality and human nature are, and thus where the researcher is coming from concerning these issues) and research methods (who the population is, who makes up the sample, how the sample was chosen from the population and why, how the data were collected and why they were collected like that, how the data were interpreted or analysed, why those methods were chosen and what was found). A good research design section could enable you to go out and conduct the research yourself, should you wish to do so. It can also give you ideas about methods for doing your own research that you might not have known about before you read the paper.

How to read the Findings

The findings can appear in two ways – either they are presented (often in order of importance) and then, in a further section, they are discussed in detail, or a finding is presented and immediately discussed, before the next finding is presented. Depending on the skills of the author, this can be the most interesting or the most tedious part of the paper.

It can be intimidating when the findings are presented in tables full of numbers. The author of the paper has assumed, as has the journal editor and the reviewers of the paper, that readers have the ability to grasp what the 'numbers' are demonstrating. They may look daunting, but the numbers are telling you how similar things are, or how different, or how they can be connected or grouped together, or where they are distinct and separate. You owe it to yourself as a researcher to put in the effort to understand what the numbers/tables are telling you. How else will you know whether you agree (or disagree) with the interpretation that the author has given the findings?

How to read the Conclusion

The last section should draw the threads of the paper's argument together, combining the aims (pointing out how they have been achieved), the findings, and what has been discussed in the literature section, to present a coherent finale. A common problem is that this section is approached with the inference of 'ending', rather than 'drawing conclusions/highlighting meanings/contributing knowledge'.

Depending on the journal, business and management papers often add a section of 'Recommendations', providing advice for practitioners who may be experiencing the research problem or aspects of it.

The weakest and least satisfying of closing sections are those which lamely summarise the paper; the most helpful and thought-provoking are those which draw the threads of the argument together in such a way that you feel you have come to the end of an intellectual adventure and have grown, however slightly, from the experience.

How to escape from reading the whole paper

If you can't bear to read an entire paper because you find it turgid, boring, pretentious, abstruse or obscure, then the conventions of paper-writing will enable you to get something out of it even if all you do is read the abstract, the research design and the last section.

Extracting value from your reading

In a sense, reading the paper, absorbing the words and the 'message', is the easy bit. Included in the notion of reading a business/management academic paper, is assessing the thing, deciding on the quality of its methodological approach, its methods or techniques, its relevance and its impact.

A major difference between reading an academic paper and reading something for entertainment is that there is a purpose to reading the paper. You have an intention – whether it is to gain knowledge, to confirm a suspicion, to add 'evidence' to an argument you are drawing up elsewhere – and the value you extract will depend on the degree to which your purpose has been fulfilled.

It is only possible to talk in generalities here because each discipline has its own indicators of impact, value and quality, and will define A Good Paper in slightly different ways.

And you as reader will judge differently – is a badly written paper with a wonderful idea that expands your viewpoint or alters your perspective a better paper than an elegantly written one that is merely reinventing the wheel?

A negative reaction to a paper is also worthwhile – without intending to, you are training yourself to compare and contrast, to widen your field of expertise, to become aware of what was previously unknown to you. It is great to feel: 'if they've published that inadequate/confused/trivial/ inaccurate piece of writing, then I should take my views and my research more seriously as something worthwhile'.

If you have read the paper from beginning to end, and if you have understood what the author intended you to understand, and if you have grown in some way from having read it – grown in knowledge or understanding, or in being able to grasp meaning, or successfully untangle difficult expression or extract the pearl of wisdom from the ugly shell that encloses it – then you haven't wasted your time. You have gained something intangible and of value.

Once you have acquired the ability to read an academic paper, practice will improve your skill, and this kind of reading should get easier, and might even move from being a chore to being something enjoyable. Even if it doesn't reach that point, you can comfort yourself that however difficult it may be to read a paper, it was far more difficult for the author to write it.

Appendix 2 Don't forget your ethics

What are research ethics?

Ethics are norms or standards of behaviour that guide moral choices about our behaviour and our relationships with others. The goal of ethics in research is to ensure that no one is harmed or suffers adverse consequences from research activities.

Unethical activities are tempting because they can make the task of researching a little bit easier – for instance, distorting what you have been told by interviewees to make a better fit with what you want to report, or leaving out inconvenient findings because they complicate the story you are trying to tell.

The current situation

Increasingly, universities are insisting that your research receives ethical approval if it involves other people. As a result, you need to build an ethical approach into the design and implementation of the research. Your university is bound to have codes and regulations to guide you. It is likely that there is also a Research Ethics Committee, and your business school will have a member of staff who acts as the school's Research Officer. You will need to put into your research proposal that you intend to apply for ethical approval if the proposal is accepted. And your supervisor should help you to fill in the required document asking for ethical approval.

The point of it all

No matter how inconvenient it is to add yet another layer of 'thinking-about' to your planning of the research, you can't deny that integrity in research is vital. Thinking about ethical issues will stimulate you to consider your own values and how you intend to integrate them into your researching.

Ethical treatment of participants

The first thing that tends to be thought of is protecting the rights of the participant. Whether you are collecting data by means of an interview, participant observation, observation or survey, the respondent has rights that need to be safeguarded. In general, you must design your research in such a way that the respondent doesn't suffer physical harm, discomfort, pain, embarrassment or loss of privacy.

You need, therefore, to make clear in the research proposal that you will:

- **explain the study benefits to the participant**

- **explain the participant's rights and protections**

- **obtain informed consent.**

Informed consent is the important aspect of person-to-person research. It is common sense that when you make direct contact with a participant, you should explain who you are, why you are doing the research and what the benefits of the proposed research are likely to be. This will put your participants at ease, and that will motivate them to answer truthfully – knowing why they are being asked questions improves the likelihood of honest responses. If you are going to offer inducements to participate, you need to ensure that they are proportionate to the task. In a person-to-person situation, whether in a face-to-face interview or on the telephone, the person can agree or refuse to participate directly. Getting them to sign a consent form will protect you against accusations of deception or coercion. In most situations, however, oral consent will suffice.

In a survey, you need to make sure that your covering letter explains these things, and you can assume that if the person returns the question-naire, he or she has consented to participate in the research.

Remember

- **You have an obligation, both moral and legal, to provide confidentiality, if that is what you have promised the participants.**

- **If you offer to provide the results of your research, then carry out your promise. Not doing so can be considered as deception of the participant (and thus unethical behaviour). You will also spoil things for any researchers who come after you as the participant has grounds for not believing their promises, and may therefore refuse to participate in their research.**

Plagiarism

Common sense will tell you that plagiarism is unethical and should be completely avoided.

Generally, plagiarism is not deliberately committed. This occurs through using someone else's ideas, words or diagrams and giving the impression that these are your own by not acknowledging whose they are, or where you came across them.

The real problem lies with accidental plagiarism, which includes forgetting to put down the reference for the information or the piece of text that you have incorporated into your own. You really do need to be extra careful. There is nothing more suicide-inducing than having your genuine work failed because you have been careless about acknowledging what someone else has said.

There is so much plagiarism about at the moment that you are going to be presumed guilty-until-you-prove-yourself-innocent, which may well be extremely difficult to do. It isn't easy to convince others, who already suspect you of unacceptable behaviour, that you simply forgot to include the reference rather than that you were trying to palm off someone else's work as your own.

It can't be stressed enough, and so here it is yet again:

1. **Find out, in as much detail as possible, what your business school defines as plagiarism.**

2. **If anything isn't clear, make sure that you get it clarified.**

3. **And once you are informed, avoid any of those actions completely, entirely, and absolutely.**

Appendix 3   Let's have an argument

You are going to hear that word many times while you are doing your dissertation, and my bet is that nobody will have taken the time to explain what the term means where academic writing is concerned. So here goes.

What is an argument?

First of all, and obviously, it is not what in our everyday lives is a dispute or violent disagreement. In an academic context, an argument is:

- **a course of reasoning by the use of evidence**

- **a series of connected statements intended to establish or subvert a position**

- **a statement of the pros and cons of a proposition or viewpoint**

- **a logical discussion or debate.**

Where your dissertation is concerned, your argument involves putting forward reasons to influence someone's belief that what you are proposing is the case. Using your argument, you are attempting to convince others of the validity and logic of how you see the matter and to convince them that they should see the matter the way you do. You are therefore making a point by providing sufficient reason or evidence for that point to be accepted by others.

Your argument is likely to contain three elements:

- **Supposition – an assumption about what is, or is not, the case or the state of affairs.**

- **Assertion – a declaration about the existence or the cause of something, with or without the use of evidence.**

- **Inference – an assertion which is based on something else that has been observed or is accepted as knowledge. Inferences tend to be used in deductive and inductive arguments.**

Deductive arguments

These are arguments whose truth or falseness is known in advance of experience or observation. (You will come across the words *a priori* – prior to experience.) Deduction tends to proceed from the general to the particular, the general to the general, or the particular to the particular.

Inductive arguments

These are arguments whose truth or falseness is made probable by the accumulation of confirming evidence (*a posteriori* – based on experience). Induction is reasoning in which statements are made about something based on observations of instances of that something. It argues that because all instances of 'Something 1' which have been observed up to this point have 'Property A', all further observations of 'Something 1' will also have the 'Property A'.

Fallacies in arguments

A fallacy (from the Latin *fallere*, to deceive) is a deceptive argument or an unsoundness of argument, or an error based on false reasoning. There are two types of fallacies:

1. **Fallacies that other people make in their arguments.**

2. **Fallacies that you can make when evaluating other people's arguments.**

It is obviously sensible to be aware of both kinds. You are bound to come across fallacies when you are reading publications for your literature review, and without necessarily meaning to, you could well introduce fallacies in your own argument.

The following fallacies are very easy to fall into:

- **trying to hide your uncertainty by using technical language or jargon**

- **ignoring alternatives**

- **referring to something without defining it clearly**

- **changing meanings**

- **using 'all' instead of 'some'**

- **only using selected instances that support your argument and leaving out instances that aren't helpful to you**

- **giving more credence to exceptions than is warranted**

- **using examples out of context or irrelevant examples.**

If you consider that your dissertation is really only a special kind of story, written in a special way, then it isn't difficult to bear in mind that what is expected of you is the production of an argument that solves a problem or a puzzle of some kind, using tried, trusted and effective techniques to do so.